The Pilgrim's Way

Taith Pererin Gogledd Cymru

A walkers' guide covering the 134 mile journey
from Basingwerk Abbey to Bardsey Island.
It follows the footsteps of travellers since the
7th century who have made the pilgrimage
to holy sites and shrines from
the Dee Estuary to the tip of the Llŷn Peninsula

Mike Stevens
Photography by John Bell

KITTIWAKE

About the author

Experienced long-distance walker, Mike Stevens has lived in North Wales for over 30 years, where he has long been a champion of local walks linked to historical sites and trails. A well-known writer of plays based on local themes such as the 1934 pit disaster, *Gresford*, notorious disturbances, *The Mold Riots* and a tale of the cholera epidemic, *By the Waters of Denbigh*, all premiered in Mold's Theatr Clwyd, Mike Stevens is a keen devotee of local history. This is his first walkers' guidebook.

We wish to thank the North Wales Pilgrims Way Committee for their kind help and co-operation.

Published by **Kittiwake Books Limited**
3 Glantwymyn Village Workshops, Glantwymyn, Machynlleth, Montgomeryshire SY20 8LY

© Text & map research: Mike Stevens 2016
© Photographs: John Bell 2016
© Maps: Kittiwake Books Limited 2016

Care has been taken to be accurate.
However neither the author nor the publisher can accept responsibility for any errors which may appear, or their consequences. If you are in any doubt about access, check before you proceed.

Printed by Mixam UK.

ISBN: 978 1 908748 39 3

Contents

Introduction 5

The Route

Basingwerk Abbey to the
 Friary at Pantasaph 10

Pantasaph to Trelawnyd 15

Trelawnyd to Tremeirchion 22

Tremeirchion to St Asaph 26

St Asaph to Llansannan 29

Llansannan to Pandy Tudur 34

Pandy Tudur to Eglwysbach 39

Eglwysbach to Aber Falls 43

Aber Falls to Bangor 50

Bangor to Llanberis 54

Llanberis to Penygroes 59

Penygroes to Trefor 64

Trefor to Towyn 68

Towyn to Aberdaron 73

Aberdaron to Bardsey Island 77

HOLY WELLS ON THE PILGRIM'S WAY

St Winefride's Well

St Bueno's Well, Clynnog Fawr

INTRODUCTION

The Pilgrim's Way is a long-distance trail of some 134 miles from the Dee Estuary to Bardsey Island, tracing an ancient route across the stunning landscape of North Wales.

Terrain The walk passes through the mountainous area of the country, and at one point reaches the foot of Snowdon itself. However the walk never involves severe mountaineering, although there is some rugged terrain and a few steep sections. There is a particularly sharp climb up the 'Coffin Path' from the village of Rowen to the heights above Penmaenmawr, and the stretch between Llanberis and Penygroes enters remote moorland which some may find hard-going. On the whole, though, the Pilgrim's Way is more a test of perseverance, and many stretches pass along river banks, through woodland, across fields and along the coastal path.

Getting back to base Each section can be walked in a day but getting back to your starting point can be awkward in an area where public transport is rather limited. You can park a car in Llanberis, for example, catch a bus to Bangor and walk the section back to your waiting car. Some locations are more difficult to manage this way. You may need to rely on the two car trick, leaving one vehicle at the destination point first, driving back to the start in another, walking the walk and then driving back from the destination to the start. This is certainly the case with more remote endpoints such as Pandy Tudur where buses are infrequent, or do not take you back to your starting point. We found the last section needed a car to reach Towyn in the first instance, a bus back from Aberdaron some of the way, and a taxi to complete the job.

Waymarking The Pilgrim's Way is well marked throughout, some sections better than others, with regular waymark plaques. Sometimes these are not always easy to spot, and often the waymark confirms your choice of direction rather than helps you make a decision. Occasionally the Way follows the line of other routes and there can be a plethora of signs. We were lost occasionally, missing a stile in a hedge here for example, or making assumptions which turned out to be ill-founded. I hope this guide will help, particularly when you cannot see your exit point on the far side of a field, for instance. Fields in particular are difficult to negotiate where crop rotation and animals obscure the exact route on the surface. Similarly the path is not always distinct on the uplands, and mist or low cloud can make navigation difficult. A compass in these conditions may help. Experienced walkers will know how difficult a route can become when visibility is poor.

You are in Wales Wales is a bilingual country and this can have an impact in different ways. First of all it is true to say that there are more people in this part of Wales for whom their first language is Welsh. And on one occasion we asked the way of a child who did not understand English and referred us to her grandfather who did. But this is rare. Spelling is a challenge. Some large towns in North Wales have become anglicised, such as St Asaph, but most smaller towns and villages have retained their Welsh, fortunately. Generally speaking this will not be much of a hindrance, but asking the way may leave you a little tongue-tied. It's worth having a practice speaking place names. This is not the place to provide Welsh language lessons, except to say that a word apparently full of consonants becomes much easier to speak when you realise that a consonant like 'w' is in fact a vowel in Welsh. There are a few useful phraes at the end of this introduction. It is also a question of courtesy to make some attempt to pronounce names correctly when talking to local shopkeepers and villagers. In this guide I have used both Welsh and English nomenclature. 'Anglesey' is now common parlance, and this is how the island is referred to in the text. 'Conwy' has now fortunately replaced the anglicised 'Conway'. Many towns and villages nearer to England, like Holywell, retain their English form.

Pilgrim's Way Passport If you are travelling the whole length of the route and want a record of your journey, you can acquire a Pilgrim's Passport from the Greenfield Valley Visitor Centre and stamp it yourself at various places on your travels. Locations of the ink pad and stamp, often involving a treasure hunt, are: Greenfield Valley Visitor Centre; Holywell St Winefride's Well Visitor Centre; Pantasaph Friary; Whitford Church [off route]; Maen Achwyfan [in a bird box by the kissing gate!]; Llanasa Church; Trelawnyd Church [on the post of the church notice board]; Tremeirchion Church; St Asaph Cathedral; Cefn Church; Llansannan Church; Llangernyw Church; Eglwysbach Church; Rowen Chapel; Aber Falls Nant Exhibition [a converted cowshed (!!) GR SH666712]; Bangor Cathedral; Penygroes Gallery Snowdon

Street; Clynnog Fawr Church; Trefor shop; Pistyll Church; Nefyn Maritime Museum; Tudweiliog Post Office; Aberdaron Church; Bardsey Island shop and chapel. The individual stamps have been designed by children from schools along the Way.

Accessibility The start of the Pilgrim's Way is Basingwerk Abbey, situated in the Greenfield Valley Heritage Park, Flintshire, North Wales CH8 7GH, with a car park close by on the A548. The nearest railway station is Flint. Arriva buses go from Flint to Prestatyn and stop at Greenfield. If you are planning to complete the Way in one continuous journey with overnight stops, it will be best to identify and even secure accommodation before setting out. Although North Wales is a tourist area, many of the locations where you end your walk each evening may not have an abundance of B&B, hostels or hotels. Similarly these end points are not always well served by public transport, certainly at the end of the day [see above getting back to base] If you intend to complete the walk by taking the boat trip to Bardsey Island, you must negotiate this at least the day before you plan to cross [see notes in the text] Once you have completed the Way it is possible to get back from Aberdaron by bus through Pwhelli. You can also pick up the train at Pwhelli, and make the rather long journey from there to Shrewsbury. If you want the speedier return by train, you will need to get to Bangor by bus and pick up main line services to Chester, Crewe and beyond.

Distances I have divided the walk up into sections which can be managed in a day. Some of these can be sub-divided over two days [eg. Trevor to Towyn with a break at Nefyn] 14 miles is the longest stretch. Speed, however, varies, and some distances will take more time, particularly those upland stretches, such as above Penmaenmawr and Llanfairfechan and between Llanberis and Penygroes. So it's hard to say how long each section will take to walk, as your own pace, weather conditions and taking time out to see the sights will all have an impact. I don't want to state the obvious, and I assume the majority of walkers on this trail will have some experience, but it's perhaps worth pointing out the need to make an early start, not leave too many miles at the end of the day when you are tired, and allow for mistakes, accidents [hopefully neither] and the availability of daylight. I'd also like to stress the shortage of public transport at the end of the day and the hazards of trying to find accommodation and places to eat.

Shrines and sights to see There are many shrines and sights to see en route, and I have included a short description in the text about most of them. Cathedrals, churches, holy wells, a Friary and abbey ruins form a cross section of the Christian heritage of Wales. There are also pagan and prehistoric holy places, a stone circle, a Celtic cross, burial mounds, not to mention natural phenomena mountains, rivers, waterfall, woods. You may want to research some of these before you set out. It's also worth pointing out that the Way passes through memorials of an industrial past, a cotton mill, a slate quarry, disused railway lines, not to mention old buildings that have fallen into disrepair or ruin, hospitals, houses, a watchtower, kilns and relics of former fishing industries. This is not an historical guidebook, but history is everywhere to be found on the Pilgrim's Way.

Rights of Way The walk follows existing footpaths and public rights of way. Wales is lucky now to have a walkable coastline, and this means the latter stages of the walk involve spectacular coastal journeys. There are many fields to cross, and paths can be hard to follow in pasture. But be assured there is a route if not an obvious path there somewhere, and I hope this guide will make it easier to find your way.

Equipment If this is your first experience of long distance walking, here are some suggestions. Old hands – please do not feel patronised! You will need good footgear, boots are recommended, as you will find it often muddy underfoot, particularly in the many fields, and stony and uneven on the hills. Raingear [this is North Wales after all] A rucksack or some such to keep your hands free and carry your supplies and equipment. You may not think you need gloves before you set out, but the weather can deteriorate without warning, so warm clothing should be available even in midsummer. Headgear is recommended, working on the adage that if your feet are cold put your hat on. Sunblock for when the sun does shine. You will be exposed to the elements for several hours in the day. A packed lunch, as you may not come across a handy shop. There is no acute need for a compass, but you never know when the mist will come down. A whistle is handy to draw attention to yourself should you get into difficulties – note the mobile phone signal is fitful in this part of the world. I said earlier there is no real mountaineering, but it is surprising how a short spell on windy hillside can feel as if it is. A travelling companion is invaluable.

Pilgrimage A pilgrimage is a journey, usually a long one, undertaken by those dedicated in their quest to reach a sacred or revered place. In this case The Pilgrim's Way will take you from Basingwerk Abbey on the Dee Estuary to Bardsey Island off the coast of North Wales. Why Bardsey Island? St

Cadfan founded a religious community there in the 6th century and it came to be looked on as a special place.

There are many shrines and holy or spiritual locations on the way, and the route has been devised to link churches, shrines, and sacred places mostly Christian, but not exclusively. The Celtic cross at Maen Achwyfan, the stone circles above Panmaenmawr, the ancient yew tree of Llangernyw have their own elusive atmosphere. The very landscape, the mountains, rivers, coast, fields, cataracts, flowers underfoot and clouds above, all seem to inspire awe and reverence. Whatever your reason for wanting to walk the Pilgrim's Way, I am sure you will at some time on your journey experience the feeling you have yourself become a pilgrim, following the footsteps of many others. This is more than a walk. But it is a walk, and a good one too. I hope that this guide will help you find your way across these beautiful stretches of North Wales. My thanks to John Bell for the photographs. As all walkers are helped along the way by the fellowship of their companions, I hope you will be as blessed in yours as I was in mine, Hugh Taylor, to whom this book is affectionately dedicated.

The North Wales Pilgrims Way Committee have approved this guide book.

PRONUNCIATION

These basic points should help non-Welsh speakers

Welsh – English equivalent

c	always hard, as in **c**at
ch	as in the Scottish word lo**ch**
dd	as th in **th**en
f	as **f** in o**f**
ff	as **ff** in o**ff**
g	always hard as in **g**ot
ll	no real equivalent. It is like 'th' in **th**en, but with an 'L' sound added to it, giving '**thlan**' for the pronunciation of the Welsh 'Llan'.

In Welsh the accent usually falls on the last-but-one syllable of a word.

Basingwerk Abbey to the Friary at Pantasaph

3 miles

A striking start to your journey, from medieval Abbey ruins and relics of the industrial revolution to the holy well of St Winefride, before crossing over the hill with stunning views of the Dee estuary and beyond, to reach the working Friary at Pantasaph.

Begin your pilgrimage at Greenfield where there is a good (free) car park off the main road from Flint, the A548, just past the high old railway bridge, on the Prestatyn side. This entrance to Greenfield Valley is also on a bus route.

1 From the rear of the car park go up the path and under a wooden arch marked 'Greenfield Valley' to reach Basingwerk Abbey. Bear RIGHT at the sign ahead, keeping the high green metal fence on your left to reach the entrance to the ruins.
Founded by the Earl of Chester in 1132, Basingwerk Abbey moved to its present site in 1157. Ruins dating back to the 12th century include arches, walls, and footings. It is possible to trace the layout of the church, the sacristy, chapter house and the monks' living quarters, all of which were added to over the centuries until the dissolution of the monasteries in 1537. The building then fell into decline, with the transept gable collapsing in 1901. Now a CADW site, the Abbey is open daily throughout the year 10.00 to 16.00 with free admission. Built in 1785 in ten weeks flat for the Cotton Twist Company, these rectangular ruins are all that remain of a Cotton Mill which employed 300 apprentices, many under the age of 10. Closing in 1840 it reopened ten years later as a corn mill, producing flour well into the 20th century. The whole of the Greenfield Valley is a shrine to a lost industrial past.

2 Opposite the Abbey entrance, on your left, lies the Visitor Centre and Museum, *open 10.00 to 16.30 from March to October.* There are also toilet facilities in the Centre. You can ask for your 'passport' here, an interesting document which you can stamp at various locations en route. Outside the Visitor Centre there is a mural depicting sights on (and off) the Pilgrim's Way.

3 Go forward to a kind of walkers' crossroads at the Old School, with the Green Pea Café over to your right. Turn LEFT and follow a path between high metal fences towards a house, with its wooden sculpture in front. Bear RIGHT to pass through a gate across the drive and reach a road. Turn LEFT.

4 Follow the signpost to 'St Winefride's Well' and walk uphill on the road. You will shortly find a

Basingwerk Abbey to the Friary at Pantasaph

valuable sitting area over to your right, overlooking a former industrial site. To see more of this interesting relic of the Industrial Revolution, a little further on look out for steps off RIGHT, which take you down to a footbridge over a stream.

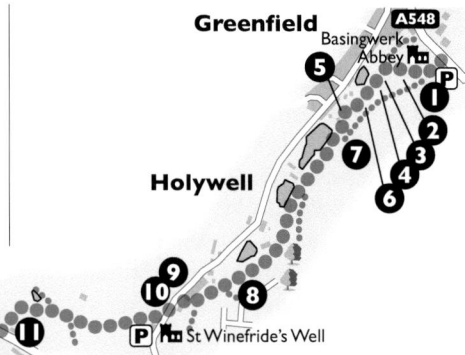

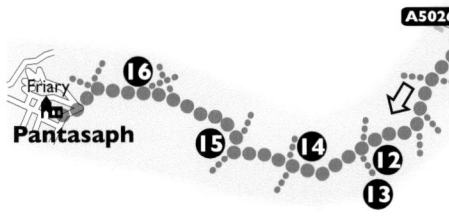

5 Once over the footbridge, wander among deserted machinery, bearing LEFT and then sharp LEFT again between ruins of Lower Cotton Mill, making for the sound of the millstream. Cross over the stream and use newly made steps with stout handrails to regain the road you were on before. Turn RIGHT onto the road. Look out for cars making their way up to the pool.

6 Follow the road up to Flour Mill Pool on your right, busy with bird life and anglers. The path divides. Carry on ahead by the side of the pool, where you will find a table and benches before reaching an old V-shaped pair of metal gates. From here bear LEFT uphill to regain the original path bordered by a metal fence and a wall.

7 Continue uphill until you reach a junction, where a wide pathway comes in from the left. Ignore a steep upward path left and also the steps down right, keeping to the broad track half-RIGHT and continue your gradual upward journey. After the useful bench on the left ignore all paths marked with posts which plunge off downhill to the right, and also the path off left up steps. Instead keep to the general upward movement of the main path. You are following an uphill broad tree-lined path, at one point with a wall to the left, making for a tall green signpost where the path divides.

8 Bear RIGHT here, following the sign to 'St Winefride's Well' and do not go off right to the Copper Battery worksite. The broad tree-lined path continues, with wayside seats, first on the right and then on the left but eventually becomes narrower, to join another path coming down from the left. Make for the black metal walkers' gate ahead. Go through this and continue down a sort of drive towards outbuildings. Veer RIGHT so that you will see the main road ahead, and with a Factory on your right reach the pavement adjoining the main road and turn LEFT.

The Pilgrim's Way

9 Carry on along the pavement past a useful bus stop to reach first The Mill on the Hill Tea Rooms, (*open 1000 to 1600 throughout the year*) and then St Winefride's Well (*open 09.00 to 17.00 April to September and 10.00 to 16.00 October to March*). There are admission charges. On the other side of the road is a small Car park, where you will continue the walk after your visit to the Well.

In legend, at the spot where Winefride was restored to life by St Bueno, a spring of clear water came flooding up from the ground. The present shrine, Grade I listed, is 16th Century late Perpendicular Gothic, although pilgrimages to the spot began in 1115. Many pilgrims, including Henry V in 1415 before the battle of Agincourt, have come before you, to bathe and benefit from the healing waters of the well.

10 Leave this car park and walk uphill along a wide stony track until it broadens out even more. Do not go sharp right over the cattle grid, but branch out LEFT uphill following a grassy track, as if making for the right-hand end house on the horizon. Cross a white dusty path and continue uphill under power lines, coming closer to a hedge on your right. The path narrows between this hedge on the right and a house boundary on the left. Continue upwards, the last stretch via steps, to reach a main road with pavements, where you turn RIGHT.

11 Cross the main road to find a small road on the other side marked Brynffynnon Terrace, where you turn LEFT. Go up this tarmac road to reach a T-junction where you turn LEFT. Do not go ahead through the gate, but instead almost immediately look out for a grassy path going off uphill and RIGHT. Follow this hedge-lined path to reach a temporary stile with a waymark. Cross the stile and continue onwards and upwards through brambles, always with the hedge to your left to reach open countryside, and a gate or gateway. Pass through, then turn LEFT and almost at once turn RIGHT over another stile with a waymark. Continue uphill, keeping close to the hedge on your left. Looking ahead you may see a stile on the skyline with power lines on poles beyond, features of the route to come. Ignore a stile in the hedge off to your left and continue uphill to a stile in a corner formed by this hedge and a wire fence. Do not go over this stile, but instead turn RIGHT and follow the line of the fence (which is now on your left) past a gate to reach a stile in the field corner. Cross the stile.

12 You now need to strike across country and uphill. Continue in roughly the same direction as before, and make your way upwards across the field, following the power lines. There is a fence to find, directly across your path, and a stile. Aim to pass, eventually, under the row of power lines as you progress upwards. If visibility is good you may also see the trig point on PenyBall Top, but perversely the route does not take in the summit, though you can make a diversion to the summit and back if

Basingwerk Abbey to the Friary at Pantasaph

St Winefride's Well

you want. Hopefully the visibility will be good, so that you can look back over the magnificent Dee Estuary, the Wirral Peninsula, the River Mersey beyond and the landmarks of both Liverpool cathedrals. Really a good sight, this, on a clear day.

13 So, once over the stile in the fence, follow the power lines upwards, aiming for a right-hand field corner on the crest of the hill, passing under the power lines now. When you reach the field corner at the top, you will find a stile, one post wearing a yellow hat. Cross here, and keep the fence close to your left as you make your way over the field to the next stile, which is to the left of a gate and carries a waymark, so you can be sure you are on the correct track. Cross the stile.

14 You are now in more rough terrain. Over to your right is a disused quarry. You can keep close to the fence on your right for a while, and then pioneer a route through gorse to make some kind of a path. Try and keep to the skyline. After a short distance a cottage ahead comes into view, and you need to make for this prominent feature. As you leave scrub and gorse, veer downhill to your LEFT, heading for the squared off left-hand corner of the property, and from here keep the buildings close to your right until you find a (very) new stile, complete with waymark. Cross the driveway to a similar new stile and you reach scrubland again. Once you have crossed over the stile turn RIGHT and go uphill.

15 You now have the cottage building on your right. Walk the length of the property and when you see the tree house in the garden, bear LEFT (waymark), following the fence which pursues a winding route and at

The Pilgrim's Way

Pantasaph Friary

the same time keeps you from falling into the quarry to your left. Keep close to the fence, but not close to the edge! Many signs on the fence warn you of the danger of falling headlong into the depths below. After a while the path passes through recently cleared scrubland and leaves the quarry edge. The path clips the field to pass between new gate posts, with a prominent tree on the right-hand side. There has been considerable work done beyond here recently, including the removal of a fence and hedge, so once you have negotiated the gateway, aim for a prominent power line pole in the middle of this large field.

16 Once you have reached the electricity pole continue in the same direction until you come to the corner of a good-sized wall facing you (with a waymark). Now you need to change direction totally, so turn LEFT and plunge downhill keeping the wall close on your right to reach a kissing gate. Go through the gate, with a house to your right, and walk down the lane, towards the churchyard. Cross into the churchyard over a stone stile, keeping the church to your right. You have now reached the next part of your pilgrimage, the Franciscan Friary of Pantasaph. Pio's Café is here, recently refurbished, *open all year long from 09.30 to 17.00 Monday to Saturday and 11.00 to 17.00 on Sundays.* There is also the possibility of staying here in the Retreat – but you would need to pre-book this. All in all a pleasant place to stop and look around, reflect and gather your thoughts. If this is the final stop for the day you can always arrange for someone to pick you up from here, as buses are infrequent. *Pantasaph Franciscan Friary – descendants of the Pennant family, who owned former Abbey land on this site, built a church here, converted to Catholicism and made provision for Franciscan Friars in 1852. The church was modified by Pugin, who also carved the reredos and statue of the Madonna and Child. It remains a working friary, retreat centre and the national shrine of Saint Pio. A path leading up the side of a wooded hill provides a setting for the Stations of the Cross.*

Pantasaph to Trelawnyd

8½ miles

From the Friary at Pantasaph through fields and woodland edge to an old watchtower, then the imposing Celtic Cross at Maen Achwyfan before reaching the mysterious windswept Neolithic cairn at Gop Hill, high above Trelawnyd, with good views of the Clwydian Hills.

1 Leave the Pantasaph Friary complex by way of the car park, using the access road, through the No Entry sign, with the Coach Garage on your left, making for the main road, Monastery Road, where you turn RIGHT. Follow a good pavement, crossing a road coming in from the right and continue until the pavement peters out. The grassy verge will then take you to a T-junction.

2 Cross this, the Babell to Gorsedd road, making for a stile with waymark almost opposite. Climb over the stile into the field and continue with the hedge close on your right and the roar of traffic on the A55 over to your left. Carry on under power lines to reach a stile with waymark in the field corner. Once over the stile make your way down through trees and bracken until the grassy path broadens out and eventually reaches a stony track. Turn LEFT here by the short post and follow the track to the main road, which you cross. You are now in the village of Lloc.

3 Continue along the 'one way' road ahead, with houses on both sides to reach a former inn on your right. Cross the busy main road here to the service station opposite and turn RIGHT, following the pavement. Ignore the first footpath sign off to the LEFT. You may spot a 'Pilgrim's Way' sign on a very tall lamppost in the hedge. After the next lamppost turn LEFT, to leave the pavement, picking up a footpath indicated by a waymark on a post. You are in a lane leading to a gate, with a house on your RIGHT. Once through the gate, turn sharp RIGHT into the trees. A delightful woodland walk follows for half a mile. Choose a righthand path where there is an apparent choice, (with a rather unsteady white post). You reach the end of woodland at a gate and a waymark indicating you turn left on the track beyond.

4 Keep the wood on your LEFT to reach a kind of junction of tracks. Choose the one ahead with a field edge and scanty hedge on your RIGHT. Pass under power lines. At the field corner there are two options, so take the righthand of the two to reach a kind of junction of paths, with a gate ahead and prominent waymarks. Go through the gate and walk along the lane as it becomes a definite bridle path, eventually reaching a main road, which you cross.

The Pilgrim's Way

The Watchtower

5 Now pick up the bridle way opposite, and you will soon reach a spanking new gate on 'The Pennant Walk', but do not go through it. Turn sharp LEFT instead to discover a stile in the hedgerow which will take you into a field. Keeping the field edge to your right, follow the hedge, which soon becomes a fence, to a gate in the field corner and Garreg Farm and perhaps a goose on sentry duty. Once through the gate you are in the 'farmyard' and need to look out for a field gate half-right and opposite, keeping the farmhouse to your right.

6 Go through the gate to follow a bridle way between hedges to reach another field gate. Once through this gate, cross the field on the diagonal and continue RIGHT uphill to reach a walkers' gate, with a waymark, on woodland edge. Go through this gate and proceed uphill through the wood to reach a concreted track, and turn LEFT.

7 Continue along this track until you come to a junction (with a mailbox on your right). Turn sharp RIGHT uphill along another access track. Keep the house, Garreg Uchaf, on your right and follow the grassy track uphill to the wood. Enter the wood and bear sharp LEFT along a forest ride for about ¼ mile. A waymark on a post, left, indicates you are near the end of this stretch, and sure enough a stile* facing you will take you out into open country. Before crossing the stile you might like to think about visiting the watchtower, even though it is not on the designated walk. If so, turn RIGHT here up to the watchtower on the summit with good views of the Dee and Mersey estuaries. The uphill path to the top bends to the RIGHT to reach the round tower, with its barred entrance and windows. A useful 'tree bench', with a flat, smooth surface, provides a good place to sit and view sea, estuary and the land beyond. That done, retrace your steps back to the

Pantasaph to Trelawnyd

in it. You are aiming eventually for two, as yet unsighted, stiles, the second one about ¼ mile further on at the bottom of the hill.

9 If visibility is good, once in the field look for a white-fronted cottage on the horizon, with the windfarm in the sea beyond. Be brave and set out as if for this far-off marker, as you bisect the field. Once over the brow, two white-fronted cottages appear in the valley below. Aim for these, and particularly the left-hand cottage. Again, with good visibility, you will see a fence crossing your route and with a bit of luck spot the stile you need to climb. Once over the stile, complete with waymark,

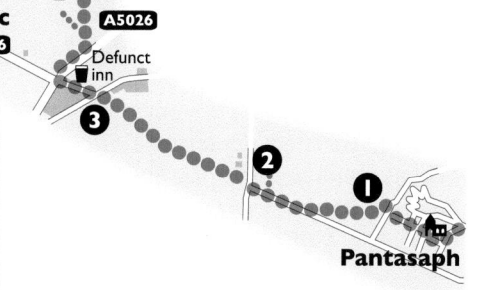

stile* and note the direction of the waymark on it.
The tower on top of Garreg Hill is a 19th century construction erected to commemorate Queen Victoria's Diamond Jubilee. It is a replica of a Roman lighthouse, or Pharos, which it was believed once stood here to guide shipping into the Dee Estuary and on to the port of Deva [Chester].

8 Once over the stile and in the field you may experience a difficult bout of orienteering. A thick sea fret obscured my vision when I came here first, and if you cannot see landmarks you may have to negotiate by compass, taking the NNW direction needed to take you diagonally downhill across the field, which may also have beasts

continue your journey across the next field towards the two cottages at the bottom. The stile you are aiming for is in the field corner, just to the right of a prominent stone wall in front of the left-hand cottage. A handsome affair, this stone stile, with steps beyond

17

The Pilgrim's Way

complete with handrail taking you to the road.

10 Once on the road do not follow waymarks which suggest turning right. Instead turn LEFT and follow the road towards a give way sign. The house on the left is now identified as Glas Coed. Once you reach the T-junction, turn RIGHT and follow the road round. The ancient stone cross you are looking for is in the field on your left, but ignore the wooden fence, which looks as if you may have to climb over into the field, because a little further on, round the corner, there is a walker's gate and an information panel supplied by CADW. Go through the gate to view Maen Achwyfan, a majestic stone cross, surrounded by its necessary, if obtrusive, protective fencing. As you come away, walkers with passports should notice the wooden box on the gate post, with its secret treasure. *Carved from a single piece of stone, Maen Achwyfan is a 10th Century Celtic cross standing some 11 feet high on its original site. The tapering shaft and small disk-head are covered with intricate carvings depicting Celtic and Viking symbols, serpents, knotwork, animals, chains and one figure holding a shaft or a spear. Possibly the tallest wheel cross in Britain, Maen Achwyfan is similar to crosses found in Northumbria and suggests a Viking presence here in North Wales, although its origin is obscure.*

11 So, after viewing the cross, go back out of the field the way you came in, turning RIGHT on the road and bearing LEFT at the road junction to find a clearly marked bridleway on your LEFT. Walking along the bridleway, you have Pen Rallt farm on your left. Pass through a gate (with waymark) and continue slightly uphill, with woodland to your right including old mine shafts clearly marked, to reach a junction of paths. Do not go through the tempting gate opposite, but bear RIGHT, to reach another pair of gates a short distance further on. Take the LEFT-HAND gate, with waymark, onto a hedge-lined track. After a short distance you pass through another gate and almost immediately a gate beyond, taking you into a field with a hedge on your left. On my last visit the field to your right was marked off with a temporary electric fence. When the hedge to your left takes a sharp turn, also left, the footpath itself goes straight on across the field, necessitating a careful rolling manoeuvre under the electric fence [!] The path then makes for a stile (waymark) in the hedge at the far side of the field, not easy to spot when you set out for it, particularly if there are cows. The stile is ahead, roughly in line with the path you have been following.

12 Once over the stile your next objective is the far corner of the field you are in, bordering the wood over to your right. A slight rise in terrain here means you cannot immediately see the stile you are aiming for. As a rough guide just get closer to the fencing, and the trees beyond, over to your right, and eventually, in the far corner, the stile

Pantasaph to Trelawnyd

appears (with waymark). Cross here into the wood and immediately turn LEFT along a woodland edge path. You soon reach a brilliant new metal gate, complete with walkers' gate to the side which you can use to gain access into the field beyond. The path now

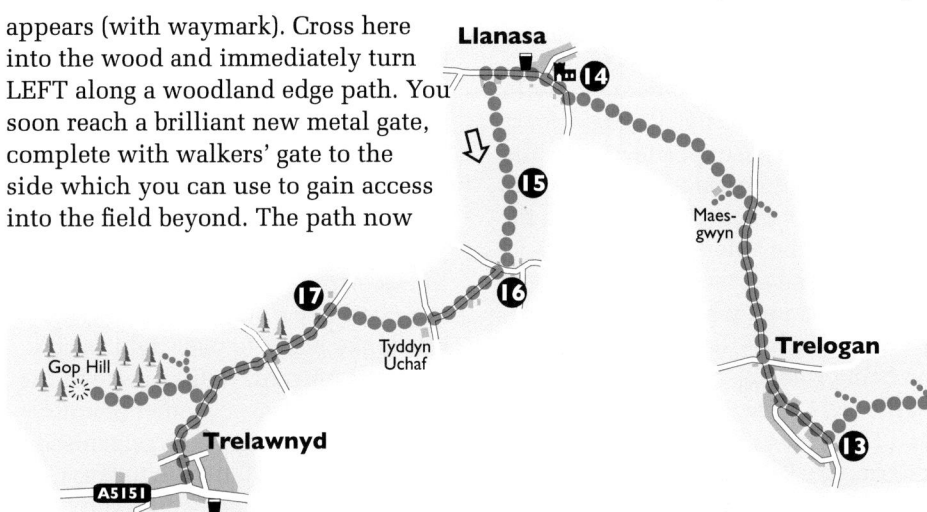

follows the fence to your left, passing under power lines to reach another radiant new gate in the field corner. Go through here into the next field, under power lines, keeping the fence to your left until you reach the next stile (with waymark) which you can use to get into the final field before the village. In this field keep the fence to your right, past the ancient Morris Minor (which will surely never run again) to reach habitation via a stile in the field corner, clipping the corner of a field over the last stile into a driveway where you turn LEFT. This track will take you eventually onto the main road where you turn RIGHT. You are now in Trelogan.

13 Quite a stretch of road work follows, as you walk downhill though the village, (you may be lucky to see a waymark on a pole on your right) passing through the cross roads with the Afon Goch pub over to your

right, and follow the road downhill. The road then climbs, and on the brow, just past the house on the right with 1887 prominently displayed, look out for a driveway, LEFT, to the Animal Rescue complex, Maes Gwyn. So leave the road and follow the driveway towards the sounds of rescued animals. You are almost in the animal rescue building before a somewhat hidden stile in the hedge on your RIGHT takes you into the adjacent field. Once in the field turn LEFT and follow the field edge, with a hedge to your left to reach the next stile. Once over the stile you need to cross this field somewhat on the diagonal, making for a hedge on your right which will help you reach a stile in the far corner. This was made more difficult to see when I crossed last, as it was occupied by a large number of somnolent cows and calves. Once over the stile in the far corner you need to cross the next field, through crops if need be, to reach a stile in the hedge opposite, just to the right of an orange-capped sign. After the stile you are in another field (with brassicas on my last visit). Make for the large ash tree opposite with a stile taking you into parkland. You are now close to the village of Llanasa, and the gate out of the field is in the hedge downhill and to your left. This takes you onto a road, where you can turn RIGHT into the village, priding itself on being well kept, and a little way on, to the right is the church of St Asaph and St Cyndern, a landmark on your pilgrimage. Passports at the ready.

14 As you leave the church turn RIGHT and continue through the village by road, making for the Red Lion pub, but keeping this hostelry on your right while you follow a road off to the LEFT, past the duck pond and village pump on your left. Before leaving the village, look out for a crafty stone stile built into the wall on your LEFT, next to a gate. Use this to gain access to a path between high fences, which screen you from view as you wander between houses, gradually uphill to discover a stile and gain access to a succession of fields. Once over the stile bear RIGHT and go uphill to gain access into a field via a stile. In this field you continue in the same direction, uphill, to cross the field to reach another stile ahead, by the side of a gate, and this allows you to traverse the next field, its hedge over to your left, to the next stile in the field corner.

15 You are now in a somewhat larger field altogether, and need to continue in the same direction you have just been following, walking through crops if need be (winter wheat in my case). You are aiming for a point to the left of what is in fact quite a substantial thatched building almost on the skyline, making for a hedge. As you approach this hedge, you will see that it is not in a straight line across the field, as it might have appeared when you set off. So keep this kinky hedge to your right as you continue upwards to find a gate in the field corner. Here is another brand new galvanised gate with cute galvanised steps built in to allow you to cross into the road beyond, where you turn RIGHT.

16 Follow the tarmac uphill, passing a post box and very soon turn LEFT off the road along a track signposted Byway Cliffordd. Keeping habitation to your left, continue uphill along a track taking you to the farm, Tyddyn Uchaf. More or less on the brow you need to cross a track to reach the farm. Keep all farm buildings to your left to find a diddy stone stile which will allow you to gain access into the field. Keep the hedge to your left to reach another stile and enter a larger field where I was greeted by rollicking bullocks, quite friendly but curious. You are making for the lane almost directly across. The best way of reaching the lane is through the field gate, but the footpath takes you over a couple of stiles to your left to clip an adjacent field. Either way, once in the lane, turn LEFT.

17 Another stretch of roadwork follows. Continue for ½ mile

Pantasaph to Trelawnyd

Maen Achwyfan

by road, passing over a cross roads and climbing towards woodland ahead. The road veers round to the left, and although you are making for the wood, keep on the road towards Trelawnyd for a short distance to find a kissing gate over in the hedge to your RIGHT. Continue now off the road and uphill to another kissing gate, and turn LEFT through a gate into the wood. A rewarding stretch of woodland walk follows, as you wind your way gradually along the edge, between trees, with good views of the Clwydian hills to your left. The path gradually shakes itself out of the wood and a sharp climb takes you to the top of the curious and exposed summit of The Gop, where you can feast your eyes on the surrounding countryside. A good end to the walk. Retrace your steps back the way you have come to the gate* on the road, and turn RIGHT to follow the steep hill down into the village of Trelawnyd.

The man-made Neolithic mound, Gop-y-Goleuni, straddling this rocky outcrop. is no small affair, measuring some 330 by 225 feet at the base and 40 feet in height. Its origins are obscure, and late 19th Century excavations revealed no burial chambers and no ditches, although commanding views suggest a good look-out position. A massive construction of limestone blocks and stone covered in earth, making it the second tallest artificial mound in Britain, Gop Hill Cairn retains an air of brooding mystery.

Trelawnyd to Tremeirchion
6 miles

On to the Clwydian Hills now, an Area of Outstanding Natural Beauty, through fields of daffodils (in season) and pet aeroplanes, with a sprinkling of the occasional dinosaur and several giraffes.

1 Walk along the pavement by the side of the main road in Trelawnyd in the direction of Dyserth as far as the zebra crossing. No zebras here – but later on look out for a dinosaur (and several giraffes). Turn LEFT off the main road, into Cwm Road, keep the church to your left and continue downhill until the lane goes over a bridge. Leave the lane after the bridge, by turning sharp LEFT at the Public Footpath sign and follow the track. Continue along with the stream to your left, avoiding the entrance to the bungalow, Swyn y Mynydd, to reach a stile. Once over the stile, negotiate your way via a post on the right along a bridle path. You are now in open country.

2 Following a path, cross over a footbridge to reach a field sloping upwards in front of you. You need to make your own way up this field (there is no path) towards some hawthorn bushes, half RIGHT. You may be able to make out a white post at the top of the field and, if so, go for it. Keeping the bushes to your right, find the far corner of the field where there is a stile, cross, and negotiate the next field by keeping close to the hedge on your left which will bring you to a brand new impressive stile. In fact there are two stiles. Cross them both to reach a track and turn RIGHT to go downhill.

3 Continue down this track to reach a gate with a stile on its right. This will bring you onto a concrete roadway, thick with mud on my last visit, turn RIGHT, keeping the untroubled pond on your left to reach a ladder stile also on the left of the roadway (with a waymark) providing access into the field beyond. Once in the field turn LEFT. Continue along the field edge keeping the (new) fence to your left to reach the next stile, also on your left. Keep close to the field edge with woodland beyond the fence. Another stile. After this stile the field you are in has to be crossed by clipping the corner. You may be able to see the next target stile ahead, giving you access into a wood on your left. Climb over the stile into the wood, 'The Flash'.

4 The path continues to a kind of woodland crossroads. Continue ahead, following the yellow marker arrows to a stile which will take you out of the trees and into a field. Go straight across this field, making for a distant left corner by clipping the edge of scrubland on your left. Once

Trelawnyd to Tremeirchion

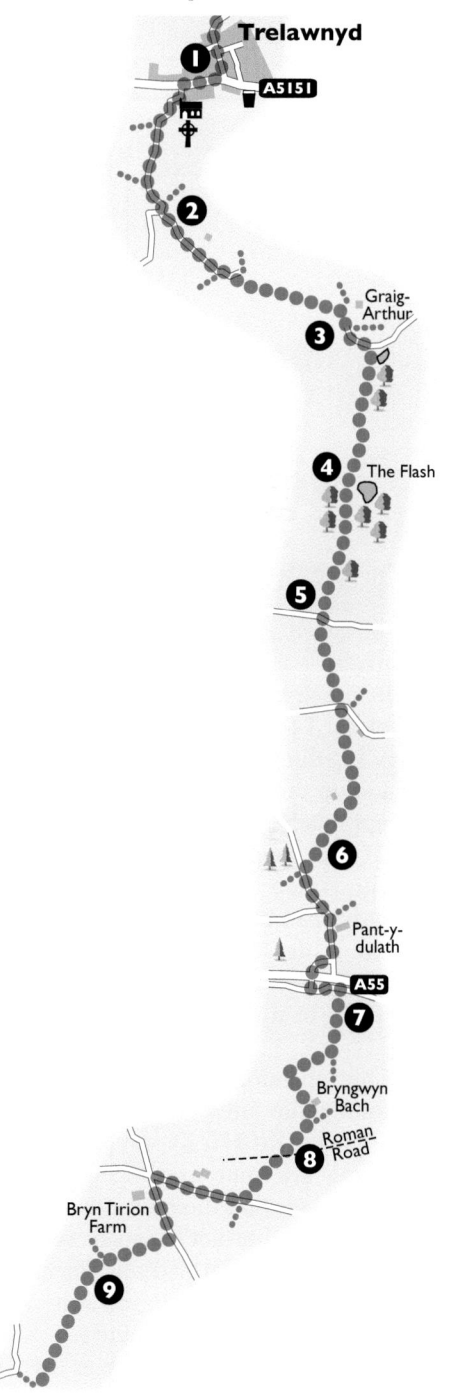

past this, you should be able to make out the stile in the far left-hand corner. You have another field to negotiate by keeping close to the field edge on your left to reach a further stile in the corner providing access into a lane.

5 Once in the lane turn RIGHT and immediately look for a stile, LEFT, which propels you into the next field. Keep holly trees to your right and traverse this field to reach a stile which will provide you with access onto a (tarmac) lane. Cross the lane to use the stile opposite. A waymark confirms the route. Yet another field faces you. The way to cross this field is to make for an electricity pole. As you approach your target you will see a stile to the right of the pole cunningly covering an electric fence, the last time I came. Once over the stile go straight across the field (are the playful horses still there?) to the next stile. Cross here into a field with trees and a fence close to your right making for a stile in the corner where you may get a welcome from dogs beyond. Go slightly uphill in this field to a stile allowing access into the next field. Veer RIGHT at this point to make for a slightly more obscure stile to the right of a gate in the hedge beyond which will bring you onto a lane.

6 Once in the lane turn LEFT and follow this for a while, looking out for a stile, LEFT, taking you into a field [surprise, surprise] which you cross at an angle. Make for the white house half right. Once you have clipped the field, use the stile to reach the road where you turn LEFT. Follow this road, a genuine road, for a

The Pilgrim's Way

Gop Hill

while, passing Glan Llyn common land and at the T-junction continue ahead following the sign to Rhuallt, passing a house on the left, Pant y Dulath. As you approach the snarling A55 turn RIGHT on a road, again signposted Rhuallt, which will take you over the main road below by means of a modern bridge. Once over the bridge turn sharp LEFT to leave the road and follow the bridleway signs.

7 Continue along this tarmac road for a while until you reach a stile in the hedge, RIGHT. By the side of the stile are some warning signs informing you that the footpath has been changed, but not to worry, no need to work out the grid references, just turn your attention to the stile and cross over. Your path here is directly across the field, more or less due south, passing oak trees in the centre of the field. The crop in the field when we came last time was daffodils! So you may have to tip toe your way through flowers to reach the far edge of the field and a stile. Here you will be greeted by two more signs, one announcing another NEW FOOTPATH and the other telling you: CAUTION AIRCRAFT MOVEMENT IN THIS FIELD, referring to the open space ahead. There may or not be aircraft, but there could be a dinosaur. To avoid aeroplanes, and dinosaurs, the new footpath takes you round two edges of the private airfield, in an anti-clockwise direction, between ancient hedgerow and modern fence, eventually escorting you out via a stile onto a lane, where you turn RIGHT, by-passing Bryngwyn Bach.

Trelawnyd to Tremeirchion

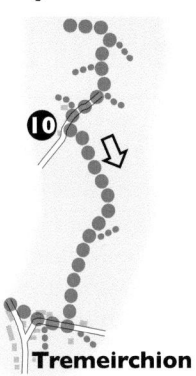

8 Walk along the driveway, ignoring a stile on your left, to reach a decorative gate straddling the drive, which opens easily enough to bring you out onto the road beyond, where you turn RIGHT. Continue along the road and at the cross roads turn LEFT, following the road uphill. This will bring you to more plastic livestock in the farm to your right, huge giraffes peering over the hedges, not to mention aliens in the driveway of Bryn Tirion Farm. Just past the house look out for a track, RIGHT, and follow this towards Penymynydd. Just before you reach the property use the galvanised kissing gate on the LEFT to gain entry into the corner of what could be a very muddy field. Walk up from here, keeping close to the hedge on your right to reach a second kissing gate, and pass through to gain more open country, gradually providing superb views of the Vale of Clwyd and the Irish Sea over to your right.

9 Negotiate the field by striving upwards to the hilltop, half-RIGHT. Once at the top of the hill keep the fence to your left to reach a stile which will help you into the field beyond. No sooner are you on the top of the hill than you need to plunge down the other side and follow the path diagonally downwards to a bridleway. Turn LEFT here on the bridleway following the signpost upwards again. For a short distance you are on the Offa's Dyke long-distance footpath, as it strides along the superb Clwydian Hills, but after a while another signpost directs you downwards, RIGHT, so descend here, ignoring a stile on the left to find another stile and gate. Over you go and down again still, ignoring a stile on the right to reach a preferred stile and gate, and beyond that the bridleway which becomes a lane.

10 When you reach cottages on this lane, go LEFT via a stile into a field which will take you along a field edge to a small fordable stream. Once on the other side continue uphill in the field, keeping the hedge to your left, noticing a redundant stile and then down to reach a dip in the field. You might have some difficulty navigating from here (as we did!) Basically once you have reached this dip in the field you need to go half-RIGHT ahead, to gain a stile in the fence/hedge opposite which is not easy to see. Once over this stile cross the next field, half-RIGHT, again by clipping the edge. Make for the church and buildings ahead. There is one more stile to be crossed before a lined path takes you onto a road, where you can turn RIGHT to find the sanctuary of the Salusbury Arms and the village of Tremeirchion.

The Pilgrim's Way

Tremeirchion to St Asaph
3½ miles

From the Clwydian Hills, an Area of Outstanding Natural Beauty, across the peaceful and pastoral Vale of Clwyd to the cathedral city of St Asaph.

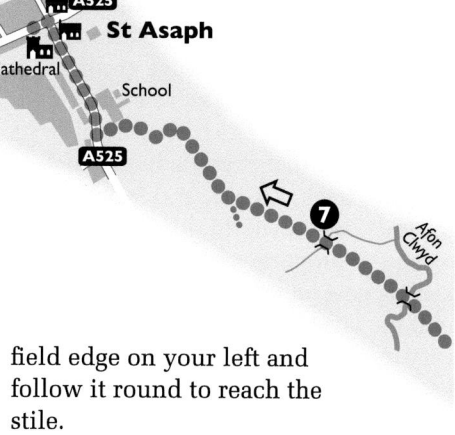

1 After leaving the Salusbury Arms walk downhill to a fork in the road and turn RIGHT. Continue along this road to take the first road off LEFT marked Trefnant. Walk along this deceptively busy road for half a mile to reach footpath signs at a property called Hafod y Coed, a building on your left. Leave the road and take the righthand footpath which follows the course of a wide hedge-lined track to reach a junction with several gates. Make for the (loose) field gate straight ahead, go through into a field and immediately turn sharp LEFT, walking under gigantic electricity pylons.

2 Aim for the lefthand field corner, with Plas Coch Farm over the hedge to your left and here find a field gate, with a waymark and a Pilgrim's Way sign. Continue in the next field to another field gate ahead. Once through into this field, continue to keep the field edge to your left, until a gate appears in the hedgerow to your left, with a waymark. Go through the gate, under the forbidding pylons, into a field sloping away from you. You need to find a stile in the bottom left-hand corner of this field. Keep close to the field edge on your left and follow it round to reach the stile.

3 This new and well-maintained stile, with a waymark, takes you into a paddock. Keep the sparkling fence on your right as you saunter down to the duck pond, on your left, where you will find a walkers' gate onto a driveway. Go through and turn LEFT, following the driveway over a metal bridge.

4 After the bridge the driveway becomes a lane and you turn sharp RIGHT uphill, directed by an unhelpfully sited waymark on a post opposite. At the top of the lane turn LEFT on a metalled road at the house Ty Gwyn and continue along this stretch to reach a main road at a T-junction where you turn RIGHT and go past, or into, The Farmers' Arms on the right.

Tremeirchion to St Asaph

5 A little further on after the pub turn LEFT down a lane, passing the sign to Ysgol Isaf on your left. Where this lane veers sharp left, at a cattle grid, leave via a stile, RIGHT, and gain access into a field. Cross the field by making for a gate between two pointers, a tree and the silo. Go through this gate. In the next field keep the hedge to your left and descend. St Asaph Cathedral beckons, over to your right. As you descend there is a ruined building over to your left and a copse. Climb over a stile, walking with the copse on your left, to another stile.

continue uphill as the path bisects a field. Another stile appears. Once over, cross the following field on the diagonal to reach a gate which will take you down onto the disused railway line, where you turn RIGHT towards the town. But not straightaway. At present a diversion LEFT takes you away from the railway line and round the school, which you keep on your right. You will soon reach the main road, where you can turn RIGHT into the town, nay city, of St Asaph, with the cathedral prominently on your left, a staging

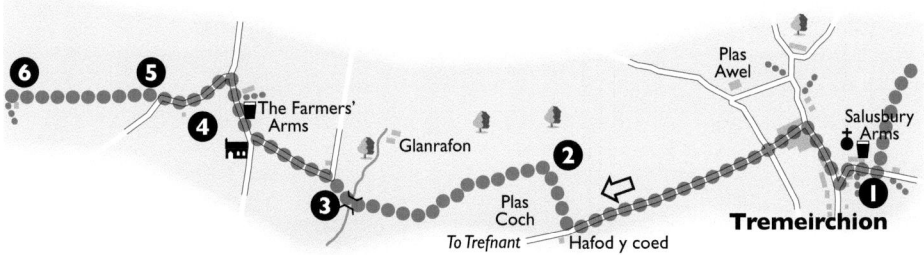

Now keep the ditch to the right to your next objective – a gate under an oak tree where you join the Clwydian Way.

6 In this large expanse of field aim for the prominent metal bridge over the river, Afon Clwyd. Once over the bridge go uphill, half-LEFT, through a gateway and under power lines to another gateway.

7 You now need to travel across the next field to an impressive footbridge under a tree. Another field. Go uphill, making for the brow, following posts on the left but keep RIGHT of the hedge to reach a stile. Once over the stile keep LEFT and

post on your pilgrimage.

One of the smallest cathedrals in Britain, St Asaph has experienced several upheavals since building began in the 13th century. Burnt down by Edward I in 1282, it was rebuilt only to be burnt down again by Owain Glyndŵr in 1402 and systematically ravaged by Oliver Cromwell's troops during the Civil War. Much of the fabric you see today is the rebuilding by Gilbert Scott in the 19th century, but choir stalls are late 15th century. On public display is the 16th century William Morgan's Bible, the first to be translated from Greek and Hebrew into Welsh.

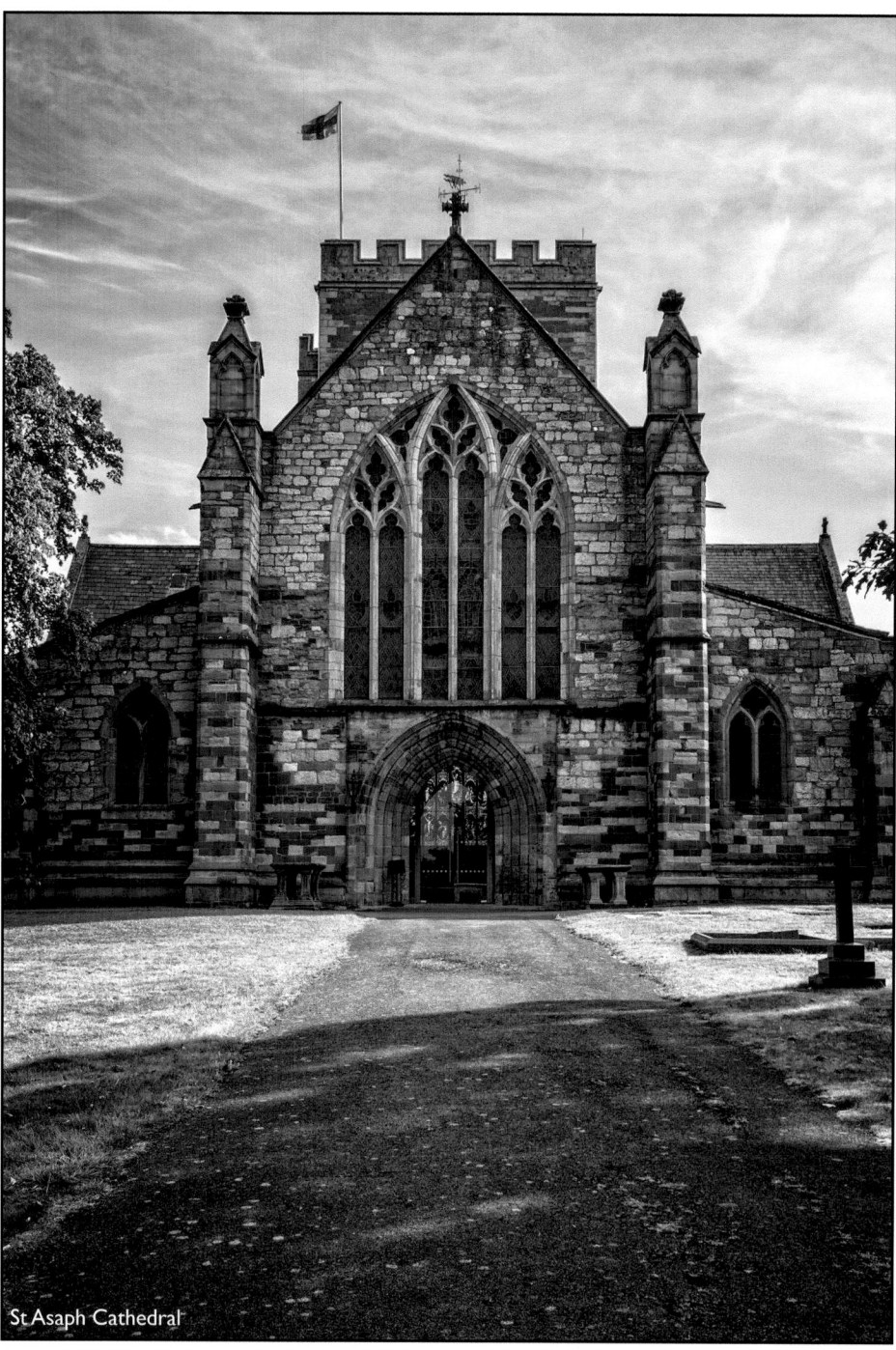
St Asaph Cathedral

St Asaph to Llansannan
11 miles

Rapid road-walking from the cathedral city of St Asaph, followed by fields and hillsides to reach a delightful valley stroll along by the River Aled.

1 From the cathedral walk downhill through the town, crossing the river, Afon Elwy, over the road bridge. You face a considerable distance of road walking now, so stride out. Once over the river turn LEFT at the T-junction to follow the Lower Denbigh Road, until the roads divide. Continue straight ahead, on the B5381, while the Lower Denbigh Road goes off to the LEFT (also the B5381) (That was my first error of the day). Pass a factory on your LEFT and look out for another tarmac road off to your LEFT, signposted 'Bont-Newydd 2¼ m'.

2 After a longish period of road walking you need to turn RIGHT where the road forks, onto a minor road, before taking the RIGHT-hand fork where this road branches. You soon reach habitation, Cefn Mairwen. Follow the road round as it curls LEFT opposite a phone box and a letter box. There is a waymark on the signpost to Bont-Newydd.

3 Continue along this road as it bends RIGHT and goes downhill. You need to look out for a hidden footpath in trees on your LEFT, just as you reach a rocky bluff on your right. This useful shortcut takes you down through woodland to reach the road again at the bottom, where you turn LEFT. Continue into the small hamlet of Bont Newydd, nestling in the valley of the river, Afon Elwy. A delightful spot.

4 Cross over the bridge, and thankfully leave the road by branching off to the RIGHT to continue happily on a track. Before long you will find a signpost and footpath on the LEFT through trees uphill to a gate with a waymark leading into a field.

5 You need to cross the field, uphill, without being able to see your destination, a gate. As you stare at the sloping field, look out for an isolated tree on the horizon, if visibility is good. To the right of this there are three or four trees together. Put them in your sights and steadfastly climb uphill. The gate comes into view now, and here you can cross into the next field. Now aim for a point to the RIGHT hand side of buildings, and make for a gate. Here there is a waymark.

6 The gate takes you into a farmyard with a slurry pit to the right and farm buildings to the left. You pass the farmhouse itself, Croen-Llwm-Mawr, on your right, as you follow the roadway down to a crossroads. Go

The Pilgrim's Way

straight across here then upwards to pass between the farm Tyddyn Bartley on your left and farm buildings on your right, making for a gate between the two. You soon come to another gate. Go through it and turn RIGHT into the field, keeping the fence to your right for a while. You should see a waymark on an electricity pole.

7 The path now follows the field edge, circling to the LEFT, close to woodland on your right, eventually leaving the field via a stile. Cross over here onto an enclosed track, turning LEFT to go through a gate as you reach Tyn y Bedw and a lane. Follow the lane to a junction and turn RIGHT downhill towards a cottage. Keeping the cottage on your right continue down through an enclosed gulley to reach a stone footbridge, more of a slab really, over a stream, and carry on up the other side.

8 Walk uphill with a fence on your left, passing scrap metal on your right until the path opens out to become a hedge-lined lane, with a cottage on your left. When you reach the road turn RIGHT and follow it for a while, going over a crossroads and downhill. After a short distance look out for a waymarked path off to your LEFT and this way gain entrance into a field, the first of a sequence.

9 In the first field keep close to the stream on your left for a relatively short distance, before turning your attention RIGHT, to forge a direct route across the field to a stile in the fence to the right of trees, with a muddy ditch in front. Cross into the next field.

10 Go straight across the second field to reach a gate which is difficult to spot, being at right angles to your line of approach, as you will only discover when you get there. Go through the gate and continue in the third field in the same direction you have been following, with a hedge on your left, somewhat uphill. A gate takes you into a fourth field, again keeping the hedge to your left. You aim now for an open muddy gateway (deep enough for frogspawn in season) and enter the next field, (this must be the

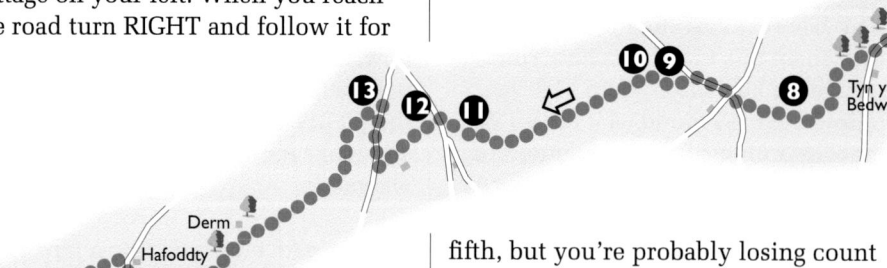

fifth, but you're probably losing count by now). Clip the field, following a right-hand inclination to reach a stile and the field beyond.

St Asaph to Llansannan

11 Once again, cross this next field on the diagonal, aiming for a gate. Go through the gate and turn RIGHT, keeping the hedge to your right to reach a field corner and a stile onto a lane. The fields are behind you, (phew!) but there are more to come!

12 Although you are now on a lane, do not use it except to cross into the field on the other side. Proceed uphill with a hedge to the right. At the gate in the corner you seem to run out of waymarks, and once over the gate (a climbing job, we discovered) you find yourself in a small field. Keep the hedge to your right and make for the right-hand gate of the two that you can see. In this final field cross to a right-hand corner and a gate which will bring you out onto a lane where you turn RIGHT. Follow the lane for about ¼ m, looking out for a footpath sign on the left which will take you off the lane and back into countryside again.

13 So at the sign turn LEFT off the lane, before it begins its steep descent into Llannefydd, to join a route now clearly marked, through a patch of gorse and over a stile on your left into a field. Suddenly it becomes unclear where you should go next. You are in fact aiming for a gate in the far right-hand corner of the field, which you can't see when you set off. Aim to cross the field on the diagonal and the gate will appear. You hope. You are now on a regular journey of field and stile, with views of Dolwen Reservoir to your right. Go downhill to a stile, keeping the fence to your right, into the next field, over the next stile, with the fence on the right, into a field on the side of the hill to a stile by a gate. Cross into the next field and hug the contours of the hill. After the next stile, keep the fence on your left going more downhill, to find a waymark on a Scots pine tree, continuing on down, past a prominent beech tree. You are now descending a little more rapidly as you pass a small copse on the left before dropping down to a farm, Derm, a gate and a cattle grid.

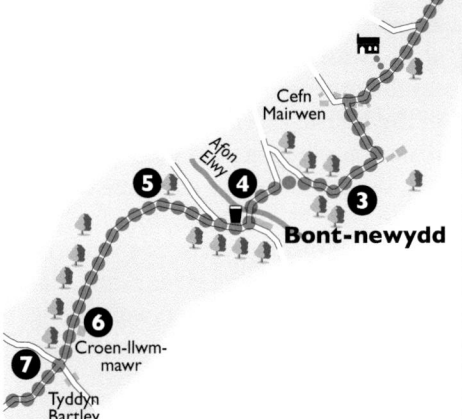

The Pilgrim's Way

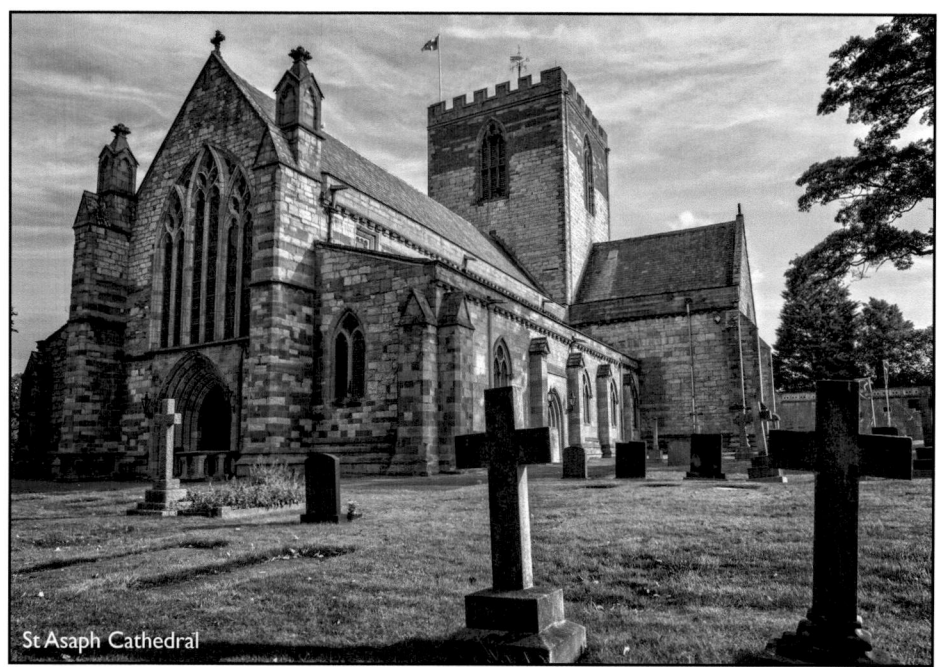
St Asaph Cathedral

14 Keep on this track over another cattle grid and turn RIGHT to Hafodty. When you reach the house, look out for a gate opposite, go through it, and once in the field keep the fence to your left as you walk downhill into the valley. You reach a stile with a waymark. In the next field you are making for a stile in the corner, diagonally, leftish, at the time of writing cunningly hidden by a fallen tree. Cross here into the field on the other side and now keep the fence on your right, continuing downhill with a steep hillside coming at you on your left. Pass a gate on the right and continue with the fence also on your right. A stile in the far right-hand corner of this field takes you to a concrete track leading to a lane. Go over a cattle grid and turn RIGHT downhill.

15 Look out for a footpath on the LEFT and join it by crossing a stile. Walk down to a stream and climb up the other side to pass close in front of the house, Cae'r Groes. After a short distance, where a path goes off to the left, do not use it but continue down to the lane, to follow another footpath down hill through trees to a footbridge over the fast-flowing river, Afon Aled. Turn LEFT after this, and walk along the valley floor, with the river to your left, venturing more to the right to pass in front of charming cottages. Just past the buildings look out for a gate on the RIGHT which will take you onto an access road, eventually becoming a lane. Cross a bridge, and once on the lane, go LEFT over another bridge. This takes you across the river again, on a firm road, to reach a small community of houses, Rhyd-yr-Arian.

St Asaph to Llansannan

16 This road joins another, the B5382, close to a telephone kiosk, where you turn RIGHT. Almost immediately you leave this main road, to follow a footpath off to your RIGHT crossing the river once again. Follow the track, which joins the Clwydian Way, up through the wood. On the brow of the hill you reach a new-ish bungalow, and the path takes you on a diversion to the left, passing close in front of the building which is now on your right. This modern building replaced the stylish First World War German prisoner of war camp (Dyffryn Aled), the scene of a spectacular break-out. Once you get back on track, follow the tree-lined driveway to cross the river for the final time. Turn RIGHT along a track with the river now over to your right, passing through two blue gates to reach the main road, the A544, turning RIGHT to gain access to the village of Llansannan.

The present-day unassuming bungalow on this site, Dyffryn Aled, replaces a massive 25 bedroom mansion acquired by the Army in 1914 and turned into a German prisoner of war camp. In a notorious break-out in August 1915, three German officers walked to Llandudno to rendezvous with a pre-arranged U-boat, but were recaptured. Nothing to see now, but a haunting reminder of

The Pilgrim's Way by the Afon Aled

The Pilgrim's Way

Llansannan to Pandy Tudur
10½ miles

Woodland edge and riverside contrast with hill-walking, as you venture onto the edges of the Snowdonia National Park. No mountains to climb, but there is more uphill work on this stretch than you have experienced so far.

1 Come out of the car park in Llansannan and turn RIGHT on the main road, with a sculpture on the corner on your right-hand side, dedicated to the memory of many prominent scholars, ministers and writers associated with this parish.

2 Take the main road for a short distance, crossing over by the 'Snooker Hall' (yes, really!) to take the road on the LEFT named Ffordd Gogor and walk out of the village. Leave the road by means of the second marked footpath to the LEFT at Fferm Gogor Ganol using the bridge over a stream to enter a farmyard. Leave the farm, (there is a waymark), and walk down the track to cross the river over a bridge. Once across turn RIGHT and keep the river to your right, hugging the field edge, crossing a tiny stream coming in from the left and, as the field narrows, using the stile in the corner to cross into woodland. A pleasant woodland walk follows for about ½ mile before dipping down to cross the river, Afon Aled, over a bright new bridge (waymark on a tree).

3 Once over the river you face a steeper incline, followed by a similar descent with the river now flowing on your right, to reach a stile onto a road, which you cross. Follow the track opposite, with the river closer now on your right and a fence on your left, until the track comes out onto a road with a former water

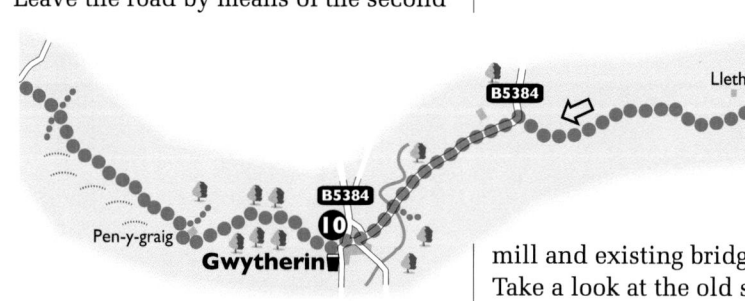

mill and existing bridge on your right. Take a look at the old structures, then turn LEFT on the road and walk up the metalled road until you come to a cross roads where you turn RIGHT.

4 Pass the homestead Acrau-uchaf on your left and at a road junction leave the road, thankfully, to find a

34

Llansannan to Pandy Tudur

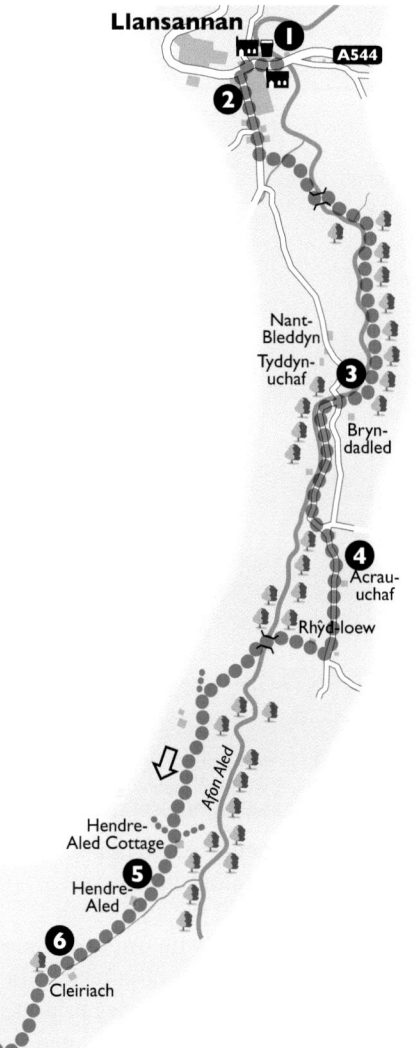

footpath off to your RIGHT which takes you down through a farmyard and between deserted buildings, (Rhŷd-loew) alive with chained dogs on my last visit. The path takes you down steeply to the river, at first close to a stream in a gully to your left. You cross a stile and once at the bottom turn LEFT to follow the river (now on your right) for a very short while until you find a footbridge. Cross over the river and take the path up quite steeply now through woodland to reach a stile which brings you into a fairly large, open, sloping field. An act of faith is now required as you cannot see the gate you are making for, somewhere up at the top. The best way is to make sure you go uphill, cutting the field on the diagonal and keeping well to the left of the gorse, if gorse there is. Eventually, as you labour upwards you will see the desired gate. Go through the gate and in what seems like an act of open defiance follow the track taking you downhill again, as if back to the river. But you do not get that far. You reach a stile, RIGHT, and gain access into a field. Hug the contours of this field as you make your way for a cottage ahead. There is a muddy creek to avoid (go above it, to your right), head for the stile and enter the surrounds of Hendre Aled Cottage.

5 Turn RIGHT after the stile and almost immediately turn again, to skirt the house and join a track with a white metal fence on your left hand side. Just on the other side are newly planted *Araucaria (monkey puzzle trees)*. They should still be there! Follow the track to the next

The Yew Tree at Llangernyw

6 Follow this roadway upwards as it bends to the left to come out on the brow of the hill and an inviting seat, known as The Pilgrims' Bench, where you can get your breath and look back at the way you have come. Good views here, but better are to come. After your rest, continue along the track, over a cattle grid, to come out onto common land. Turn RIGHT here and go uphill on the road for some distance, over a cattle grid until you reach a road junction. Suddenly marvellous views of the Snowdon range appear on your left, rearing up as if out of the ground, snow-covered on my last visit. When you reach the road junction, turn LEFT, and follow the road until you come to another junction where you turn RIGHT. This next road, or lane rather, continues for a while, with Tan-y-foel to the left and Tynyffynnon to the right, and you need to leave it where it bends sharply to the right at Tŷ-nant. Here go through a gate on your LEFT to gain more open country again, a blessing on your feet. The track wends its way round and uphill. There follows a change of direction which is not too easy to identify. The track you are on goes up to sheep pens, but do not go that far. Instead turn RIGHT, apparently aimlessly.

homestead, Hendre Aled, and as you go past, or rather between the buildings, look out for a footpath sharp LEFT, with a stile, into the field. Follow the field edge to the next stile and cross over into a somewhat larger and shapeless field. Now you need to continue uphill, keeping trees to your left and making for a lone tree in the field itself, which you pass, keeping it on your right. Continue upwards to a field corner, where there is a stile with a waymark, and cross into the field beyond. There is a gully and stream to your left, acting as a guide to reach a stile out of the field, where you turn RIGHT onto the access road.

7 Clip the field, making for a gate in the fence. From here your path is downhill with the stream flowing close on your left. This path will take you down to another deserted farmhouse, Hafod-gau, in the dip, surrounded by conifers. Leave the track, turning LEFT through a gate and cross in front of the ruined farmhouse to find another gate on your right-hand side. Now go uphill, without a clear view of your exit point from this field, which is to be a stile. This becomes clearer as you climb. Once over the stile you are in a lane, which you cross directly, to climb a stile on the other side, with a reassuring waymark.

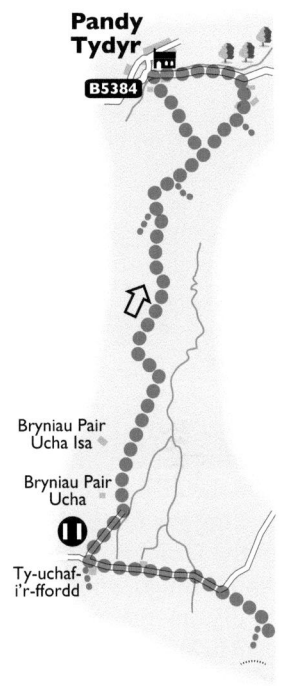

8 In this field, keep the fence to your left then cross over a stile, a footbridge and another stile. You are now in a much larger field and have a steep gully or ravine ahead to navigate. It's probably best to find the sheep path, slightly over to your left which will take you through gorse and scrub to the stream at the bottom of the gully and up the other side where there is a broken gate and a waymark.

9 Once in the field at the top, cross it on the diagonal, moving away from the fence on your right to gain a gap in the hedge ahead. Cross the field to a gate, and over another field to another gate to reach a lane. Here you turn RIGHT. Almost immediately turn LEFT along the road as if towards the farm at Llethr, but look out for a footpath which will take you LEFT to a kissing gate. Cross here to a gate in the fence on the LEFT. Keep the fence to your right to a gate and beyond that a slightly slippery descent to a stream (I fell over). Leave the stream on your right as you traverse the field, going slightly uphill through a gate to walk across the field to the hedge. Continue with the hedge on your right through a gate into another field and over a stile. Go initially straight ahead but almost immediately LEFT to continue, via a stile, over a low hill. Bear slightly RIGHT and head for the skyline and a stile in the hedge and fence. Turn RIGHT here and continue across another field to reach a lane. Now turn LEFT on the main road and down to the delightful village of Gwytherin, with its welcome facilities, a central seating area complete with anvil, excellent toilets and nearby the Lion Inn. All in all definitely deserving its 'Best Kept Village' award, and a pleasant stopping place.

The Pilgrim's Way

Meini Hirion

10 Leave the village of Gwytherin by taking the footpath uphill to the right of the Lion Inn. This is quite a steep climb through woodland. You will eventually emerge into a field which seems to encroach from your right. Continue uphill now, making for the derelict farmhouse of Pen-y-graig. There is a stile to the left of the building which will allow you to gain access into the field beyond. Immediately turn RIGHT to pass behind the building and reach another stile which takes you down onto a track. Turn LEFT and follow this track up to the brow of the hill where it bends right.

11 Turn RIGHT here and go through a gate (with waymark) to the lane. In about 75 yards cross over, LEFT, towards a fence on your left and follow this downhill to reach a kissing gate which will bring you to a stile in the fence and a road. Turn LEFT on the road, which you follow to a kind of crossroads at Ty-uchaf-I'r ffordd. Here you turn RIGHT. Follow this lane, passing the farm Bryniau Pair Uchaf on your left and its sister farm, Bryniau Pair Isa. Here do not go left into the farm, but continue through the gate ahead. The path takes in three more gates before deciding to adopt a sharp left-hand course. Aim for a gateway with conifers. Pass the conifers on your right and immediately turn RIGHT, keeping this copse also on your right. The pathway here is somewhat obscure, although there are waymarks on posts, with arrows, in the field. You need to make for an exit point leftish across the field you are in. The path, if path it is, veers to the LEFT and comes out via a gate onto a bridleway which itself becomes a lane. Look out for a gate on your LEFT and go over a stile down to the village, or if you are weary of stiles and fields at this stage in the day, continue on the lane to reach the B5384 where you can turn LEFT along the main road into Pandy Tudur.

Pandy Tudur to Eglwysbach
10 miles

A pleasant walk across fields, by the side of streams and through woodland, to visit one of the oldest surviving trees in Europe, before entering buzzard and red kite territory and on to the village of Eglwysbach, close by the glorious gardens of Bodnant.

1 Cross the road bridge in the centre of the village of Pandy Tudur heading west, and turn RIGHT up a sharp narrow road (marked as unsuitable for HGVs) At the top turn RIGHT along the lane. Follow this lane, passing the converted church and vicarage, now a nursing home on your right, descending to the A548 where you turn RIGHT.

2 Walk along this busy road with care, to follow a lane on your LEFT leading up to the farm, Llwyn Du Isa. When you reach the farm, pass between the house and the farm buildings, veering slightly RIGHT to be faced with three field gates. Take the middle one to gain entrance into a hedge-lined lane. At the top, cross over, RIGHT, via a stile (with waymark) into a field. Your exit point from this field is a stile in the hedge on the far side, next to a prominent tree. Cross here and clip the next field, making LEFT for a gate which leads onto a lane, where you turn RIGHT.

3 After about 100 yards look out for a footpath on the LEFT which will take you down a muddy track as it bends to the right and comes out onto a large field. Keep close to the field boundary on your right for a short distance until you reach a gate also on your right and here change direction. Now you need to cross this large field on the diagonal to reach a ladder stile, as yet unseen. Aim to walk with the woodland of conifers well over to your left and cross the field, passing through an old field boundary with the remains of trees. Do not despair, as the stile is down there in the bottom corner, somewhere, hidden behind trees. Cross over this tall, handsome ladder stile, and by clipping the field corner reach a stream which you can cross via a concrete (untypical) footbridge to enter a wood.

4 A very pleasant woodland walk follows, with the stream a constant companion on your right-hand side. There are sturdy footbridges with good handrails and at times steps cut in the rock. The path opens out at one point to reveal a wooden sculpture area with benches and appropriate sayings in English and Welsh, and then continues its descent through a picturesque wooded gorge, which is often wet and muddy, even in dry seasons. After your constant descent, the path climbs up for a short distance with a

The Pilgrim's Way

walled garden on the right, and you come out onto the drive to Hafodunos Hall, a private house. Turn RIGHT along the drive and RIGHT again at the Lodge, which is being renovated, to take the road, and proper pavement, into Llangernyw.

5 Here there are plenty of facilities, a shop, the Old Stag 17th century Inn and most amazing of all, in the churchyard of St Digain's, the Yew Tree.

Flourishing in the graveyard of St Dygain's, a male yew, over 4000 years old, is one of the oldest living trees in Europe and one of the 50 most important trees in Britain. The area was possibly a pagan site predating the church, and the tree is associated with several mysteries and prophecies. Legend has it that the Angelystor [the Recording Angel] can be heard there on Halloween, booming out the names of those parishioners who will die in the forthcoming year.

So pay your respects to the tree and leave the village the way you came, up the road as if back to Hafodunos Hall.

6 Just as you leave the village, however, look out for a track after the last cottage on the RIGHT, to take you uphill, through a gate and into open countryside. You are approaching the farm building of Crei, which you will soon discover is yet another deserted farmhouse. Go close to the building, standing among a cluster of isolated trees, and then continue upwards onto open country again. Aim for the brow of the hill and a line of electricity wires coming across, and more particularly a fence going upwards from trees on your left. It's probably best to locate the fence and then follow it upwards until it turns sharply left.

Here change direction, LEFT, follow the contour of the hill and keep the fence on your left and gorse on your right as you negotiate the hillside. The path maintains height and then uses a stile to cross into gorse and scrubland before descending to a lane, where you turn LEFT and follow the tarmac.

7 A disappointingly long period of road walking follows, perhaps as much as 2 miles, which can be hard on the feet, although traffic is light. Marching would be good. Singing, too, if you're up for it. You come to a T-junction, where you turn RIGHT and eventually reach a major road, the B5113. Cross over here and take to the

Pandy Tudur to Eglwysbach

road again, passing isolated cottages at Gosen to left and right until the road begins a sharp descent. We stopped for lunch here, by the roadside. The road veers right on this hill, and at this point you need to look out for prominent signs pointing towards a cattery and follow this road, turning RIGHT.

red kite, both of which birds may be spotted here. We saw a buzzard, but not a red kite. Just before you reach the house turn LEFT, pass in front of it, and keep other buildings on your left. The path continues now on the level, and you veer LEFT, if anything, towards open countryside again and a stream to be crossed.

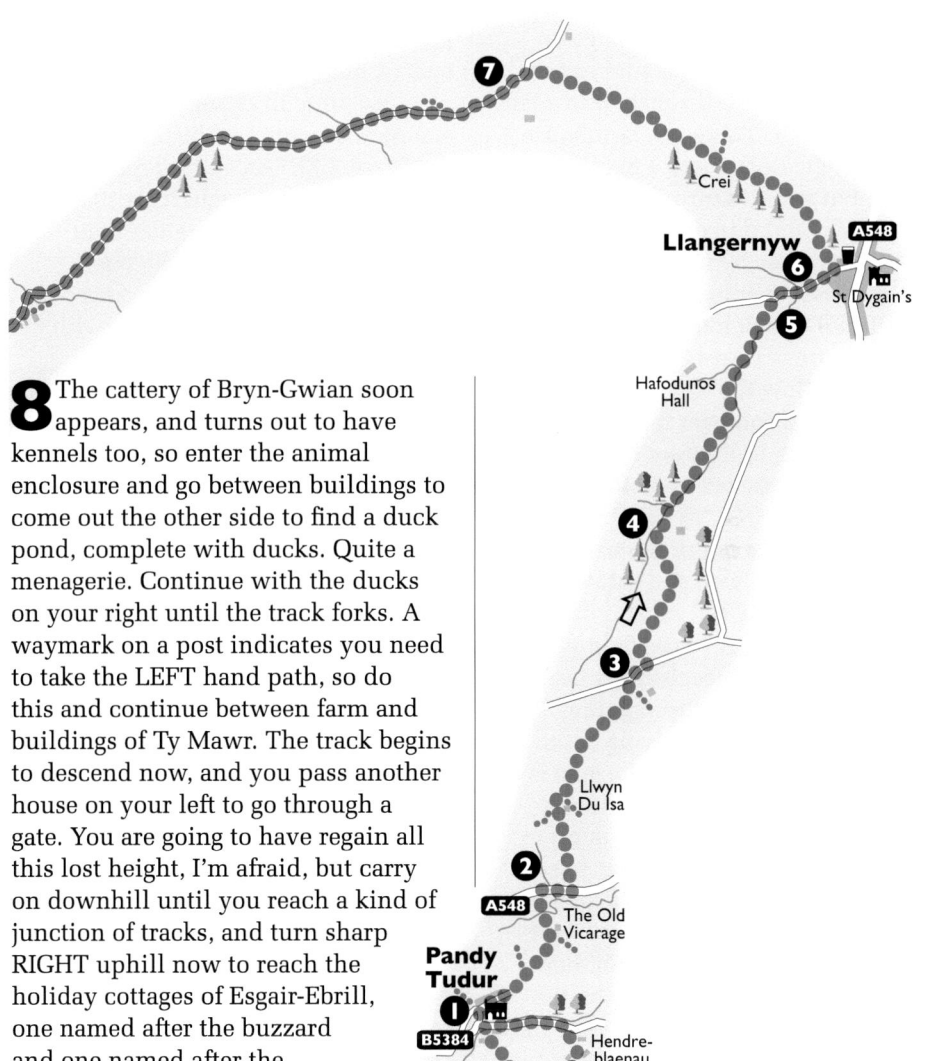

8 The cattery of Bryn-Gwian soon appears, and turns out to have kennels too, so enter the animal enclosure and go between buildings to come out the other side to find a duck pond, complete with ducks. Quite a menagerie. Continue with the ducks on your right until the track forks. A waymark on a post indicates you need to take the LEFT hand path, so do this and continue between farm and buildings of Ty Mawr. The track begins to descend now, and you pass another house on your left to go through a gate. You are going to have regain all this lost height, I'm afraid, but carry on downhill until you reach a kind of junction of tracks, and turn sharp RIGHT uphill now to reach the holiday cottages of Esgair-Ebrill, one named after the buzzard and one named after the

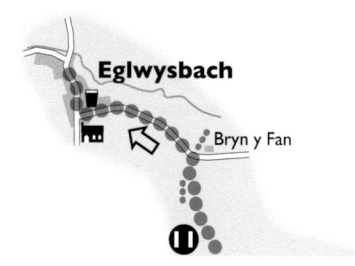

9 Once again you are in more open country but need first to negotiate a field with a well-defined track. A pylon in the distance provides a good point of reference. Maintain your height. Go through a gate with a waymark, under power lines. The path takes you as if to a gate, with a waymark on it indicating that you need to go RIGHT and not through the gate. So carry on with the hedge on your left until you reach a loose gate in the field corner. Go through onto a lane and turn LEFT. There is a farmhouse on your left, Ty Du, and a field gate in front of you. Go through the gate into a field and descend sharply with the stream close by on your right. It's not long before you find a walkers' gate, RIGHT, which takes you out of the field and across a footbridge into a wood. Follow the delightful path through the wood over footbridges and skirting young holly trees bringing you to a walkers' gate onto a field.

10 You come out of the wood through a gate and into a field. Go diagonally RIGHT, making for an electricity pole. Leave the field via a gate and you have reached the farm Llwyn-du. Continue through the property and then slightly uphill to reach a lane. Turn LEFT. The lane is very steep to begin with, but levels out. You are looking for a track off to your RIGHT which is not easy to spot (we missed it) and has no waymark. The best thing to do is look out for two gates opposite each other on either side of the road. Use the gate on the RIGHT and follow the track, with gorse tumbling down on your right. Plenty of gorse in flower this year. Mention is made of this area being a disused quarry, but this is not apparent. Another difficult change of direction emerges. You are looking for a stile in the fence, LEFT, not very prominent, with a waymark tantalizingly placed on the step of the stile rather than on a post. Further along the track, by the way, you will come across an apparently blocked off stile with a waymark on it. This means you have gone too far, as we did. I guess we were tired at the end of the day. I understand plans are afoot to deal with these problems by creating an alternative route.

11 Once successfully over the correct but impoverished stile turn RIGHT and follow the contours of the hillside along a sheep track towards the final farm, Bryn y Fan. Go between farm buildings to the lane and turn LEFT down into the village of Eglwysbach and its various amenities. You are also not far away from the glorious gardens of Bodnant, a National Trust property, and if you have a chance to visit while you are here, this is a different and rewarding shrine, dedicated to the glories of trees and shrubs and flowers.

Eglwysbach to Aber Falls
14½ miles

Crossing the delightful Conwy valley, you will climb upwards along the ancient coffin path to reach the impressive stone circles above Penmaenmawr, before a second climb takes you up to the Roman Road and down to Abergwyngregyn.

1 Follow the main road out of Eglwysbach towards the church, passing a side road on the left, Heol Martin, turning LEFT at the ancient garages to follow a lane (waymark). Cross the stream over a stone footbridge and pick up the path on the other side of the water, reacting with horror to the sign which reads, 'Your dog could be shot if....' Re-cross the stream over a similar stone bridge with metal handrails. Continue uphill on the lane now, with hedges on both sides, bearing RIGHT where it forks (waymark on a post) and follow this track.

2 The track turns into tarmac soon, after a tempting bench, so continue along this driveway, downhill to reach a road, where you turn LEFT. After Ty Gwyn the road forks, so take the LEFT hand route signposted to Tal-y-cafn, walking uphill. Good views of the river, Afon Conway as you reach the top of the hill. Ignoring turns off to the left continue along this road, downhill now, to reach the main road. Go more or less across at the crossroads to the level crossing and the railway station at the side 'Tal-y-cafn and Eglwysbach'. Follow the road towards the bridge, marvelling at the presence of a tailor's shop, right, in the middle of nowhere, and cross the bridge over the river, Afon Conwy.

3 Ignore a turning off to the right and follow the main road as it winds uphill past houses on the left, discarding the offer of a footpath signed on the left. You are looking for a lay-by almost on the brow of the hill on the right-hand side where you can turn off, RIGHT, to discover a ladder stile (easily missed) taking you into the field beyond, the first of many. In fact it's hard to keep track of them all.

4 In the first field go straight across with an open ditch on your left to a ladder stile taking you into a copse. A short muddy walk, wet enough for marsh marigolds, and a walk between trees (one fallen) brings you to another ladder stile and a second field. Keep close to the field edge now and reach a ladder stile into the third (waymark). Keep the field edge to your left as you cross, to reach a ladder stile, and the fourth field, before negotiating a low wall. Now aim for the ladder stile to the right of the tree ahead and in the next (is this the fifth?) field bear LEFT, aiming as if to the right of a pylon ahead. A ladder stile becomes visible as you reach the brow of the hill in this field, next to an electricity pole. Fields are behind you now, for the next field aim to skirt the corner of an intruding boundary hedge which comes in from the right, to gain a gate (waymark) also on your right as the path continues more uphill. Head across this field, leftish if anything, making for the left of a copse. A gate to the left of the copse takes you onto a track towards Glyn Uchaf, bearing left into the property, with farmhouse on the left and buildings on the right. There is a useful sign on the barn. Walk between buildings down the drive to the lane.

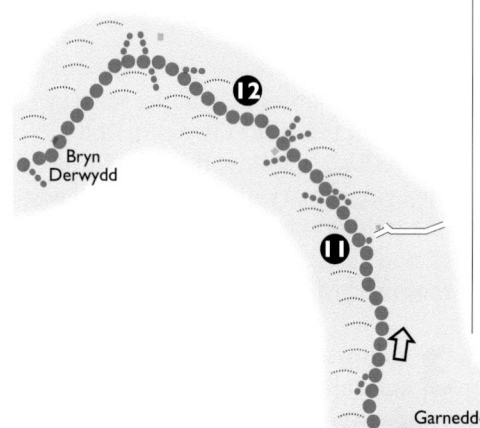
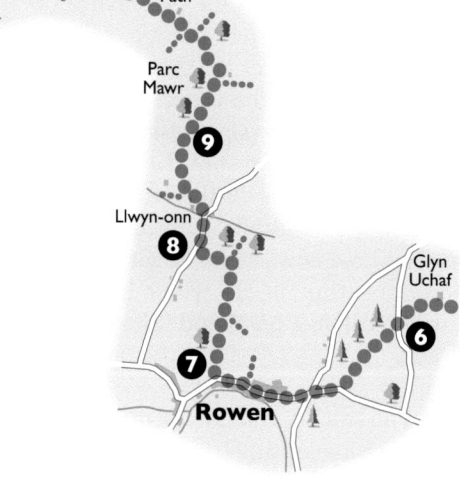

a while. Once over the ladder stile you are on a road, next to a bus stop, where you turn RIGHT. Follow the main road, LEFT, the B5106, quite busy with traffic the day we walked, until you reach a footpath signed to the LEFT, about 100 yards ahead. Take this path.

5 Keep the hedge and wall to your right as you negotiate muddy terrain, making for the farmhouse ahead. A gate (with waymark) on your RIGHT takes you into a small field, with new born lambs on our visit, to reach another gate which will enable you to pass to the right of the farmhouse. A gate on the RIGHT in the garden takes you to another gate on the RIGHT. Carry on bearing RIGHT to navigate a gap in the hedge where you turn sharp LEFT. Keep the hedge to your left and look out for a ladder stile in the far corner of the field. In

6 When you reach the lane go straight across through a kissing gate into a field. Aim for a spot to the left of trees ahead. When you reach this copse there is one tree sporting a waymark, directing you onwards towards the field fence on the right, where a ladder stile in the right-hand corner takes you into woodland edge.

Eglwysbach to Aber Falls

Almost at once a second ladder stile helps you out onto the road where you turn RIGHT. This downhill road leads directly into the village of Rowen, with its distinctive pub and tea rooms, Ty Gwyn, and chapel, where you can have your passport stamped again. If you want to break up the long walk, Rowen is a good place to stop, as the next section is fairly long and demanding. However, if your loins are suitably girded, press on.

7 Leave the village by following the road through, past the chapel on your right to find a footpath eventually off to the RIGHT between cottages. By walking through a gateway you take in a farm and gain a track with a camp site on your left and a new stile, if required. You now need to cross this field by making for its opposite corner. The path is slightly ambiguous. You can keep to the two left hand edges of the square field, or walk diagonally across, or go ahead and turn LEFT again. Whichever way you take, you will eventually reach a gate and a ladder stile (with a waymark) taking you into a lane, or track, where you turn RIGHT. As the lane/track swerves right use the stile, LEFT, to maintain your current direction. Leave the lane and cross into a field (waymark). Once in the field keep the wall to your left to reach a stile in the corner and cross into the next field. Ignore a tempting footpath off to the right, and keep to the right-hand edge of the field following a stony route upwards. You are now starting on what will prove to be a good long stretch of uphill climbing, strenuous at times.

8 Leave the field you are in via a walkers' gate and turn RIGHT in the lane. As the lane bends right to Llwyn Onn go LEFT instead, uphill, following the track with the house on your left. The walk becomes steeper. You are looking out for a large ladder stile on the RIGHT. You will know why it's called large when you see it! Use this to climb steadfastly into the field. Walk diagonally, upwards, across the field to a gate. You are close to a wood on your left and a cottage on your right, and need to enter the woodland (Parc Mawr) on your LEFT via a stile.

9 A delightful walk through protected woodland follows, alive with primroses, violets and

45

The Pilgrim's Way

early bluebells on my last visit. At a junction of tracks take the LEFT-hand one, uphill, which gradually become quite steep. This is known as the Coffin Path. Hard going for walkers, it must have been even harder for the mourners to carry their burden up this hill to the church at the top. But up it continues, crossing a track to persist uphill through a walkers' gate to bring you out of woodland eventually. Cross a stream and continue upwards with walls on both sides until you reach the end of the Coffin Path and find the gem of a church, St Celynnin.

The steep coffin path leads to St Celynnin's church, high up in the foothills of the Carneddau range and also one of the oldest churches in Wales, parts of the building dating from the 12th century. Many interesting artefacts inside include a 15th century rood screen. Outside, in the churchyard, pilgrims can also discover a holy well.

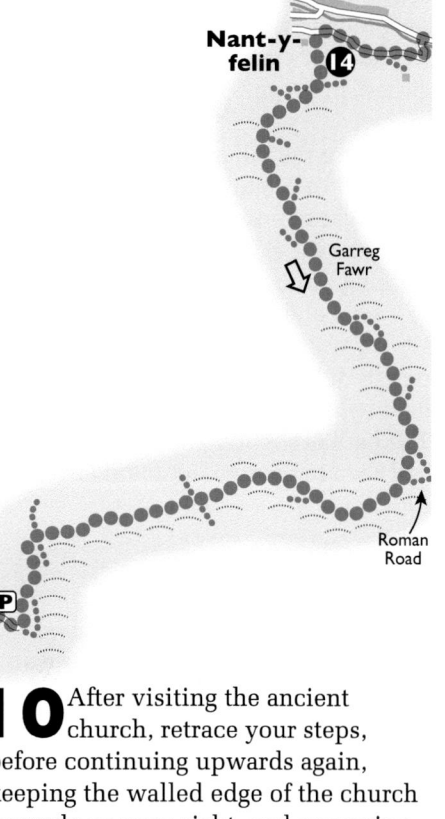

10 After visiting the ancient church, retrace your steps, before continuing upwards again, keeping the walled edge of the church grounds on your right, and appearing to aim for a house, Garnedd-Wen, also on your right. However, do not go to the house nor take the level and tempting path to your left, but continue ever upwards through a gate close to sheep pens (waymark) and onto extensive moorland fields. If the path appears to fork, take the

Eglwysbach to Aber Falls

right-hand version. You are aiming for a point, half-right, where apparently three walls meet. As you get closer you will see there are in fact four walls, and there is a waymark on a post to confirm you are on target. Cross a stream and in the next moorland 'field', if field it is, veer RIGHT, keeping the wall on your right and follow the distinctive path, more on the level now, you will be glad to know. Superb views here of the Conwy Valley and beyond. Not a bad spot for lunch, if weather permits. You are aiming next for some substantial walled sheep pens.

11 When you reach these sheep pens you need to change direction, and the next section of the walk is not easy to follow, particularly if there is mist or low cloud. At the sheep pens you need to turn quite definitely LEFT, apparently at random. Head off onto open terrain, slightly uphill as you go. The pathway can be indistinct. Even in good weather this is a tricky manoeuvre. As you reach the brow of the hill, things become clearer in good visibility. You should see a flat-topped hill in the distance. Aim for that as a guide. Once on top you should also see a clump of trees enclosed in a wall, your next target. Pass these trees close on your left, with a ruin in there, (look out for a

Aber Falls

The Pilgrim's Way

waymark) and walk down to a stream which you cross on a broad footbridge.

12 Once over the bridge a ladder stile takes you into more open country, underneath power lines, across stepping stones, (look out for tadpoles, in season) Continue uphill with a wall on your right, a waymark on a post, keeping left and upwards (under power lines again) to reach a gate which brings you out onto a well defined track. You are in fact joining the North Wales Path now with a good surface and alternative waymarks. Turn LEFT. After the last stretch of rather ill-defined pathways, the next section is positively clear and easy to follow. Keep the wall now on your left to pass the next building on your right-hand side, with pine trees and a waymark on a post. This clear path is now taking you to the ancient and atmospheric stone circles above Penmaenmawr by way of a slight diversion from the official North Wales Path. After visiting the stone circles, rejoin the main path, westwards, until the Wales Coast Path takes its own route off to the right. Pilgrims, though, continue forwards, more downhill now, through a gate to reach a gated farm, Blaen llŵyn. Follow the farm track which becomes a lane to a T-junction where you turn LEFT, at Plas Heulog.

Meini Hirion [Long Stones] above Penmaenmawr consist of some 30 stones, 11 still standing, forming a circle high above Penmaenmawr. Named a Druid Circle in the 19th Century, a tentative date for construction is given as 1450-1400 BC [Bronze Age] but a date even as early as 3000BC has been suggested. Excavations in the 1950s uncovered a burial chamber, food vessels, a bronze knife and the cremated bones of a child.

13 You are now descending more rapidly on the road as it bends its way down to the Nant y Coed Nature Reserve, ignoring any footpaths off to the left. Just after you reach the entrance to the Reserve, which is on your left, look out for a way to leave the road, LEFT, crossing a stream via a footbridge and then bear RIGHT to follow a road (Valley Road) which eventually becomes Terrace Walk, on the edge of Nant-y-felin. Ignoring footpaths to the left use, instead, a metal kissing gate in the wall LEFT, and leave the road. You are now in for another spell of hill-walking, and if this comes at the end of your walking day, brace yourself for the climbs ahead up Garreg Fawr.

14 You are now in a field, and need to make for the farthest corner, on the right hand side where a gate takes you into a walled path and eventually into open country. The climb begins. Follow the path, onwards and upwards, with occasional posts in the ground illustrating the route until it reaches a ridge, turning slightly RIGHT to follow a more level course [the Roman Road] towards gigantic pylons. The climb is over and it is downhill now all the way to Abergwyngregyn. So take the RIGHT-hand route at the walkers' signpost and continue downhill until

Eglwysbach to Aber Falls

Aber Falls

the path becomes a road. You reach habitation and a car park [excellent toilet facilities at the top car park]. If you walk on down to the village itself you will come to various facilities including a bus to Bangor, though getting back to your starting point [Eglwysbach] may be impossible by bus, particularly late in the day. We used the two car trick here. This is the longest stretch on the Pilgrim's Way, but it is possible to break the journey at Rowen or by going down to Penmaenmawr and then back again another day.

The Pilgrim's Way

Aber Falls to Bangor
12½ miles

From the spectacular waterfall you take a high rise walk along the hills with splendid views out to sea, Puffin Island and Anglesey on your way to the cathedral city of Bangor.

out for additional waymarks. Through another black gate the path keeps to the contours of the hill before reaching a second waterfall. Cross the stream via the bridge and continue down the other side of the valley now in a northerly direction.

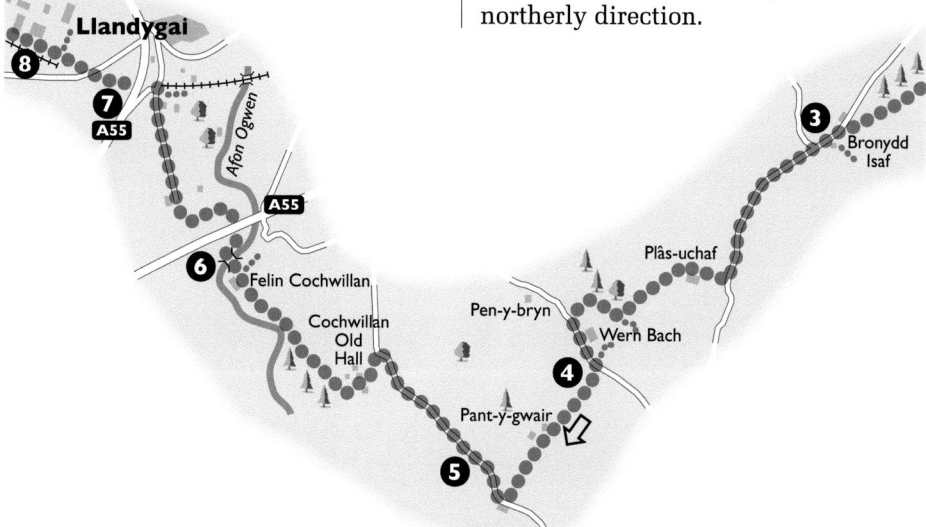

1 The starting point for this section of the walk is the car park up from the village of Abergwyngregyn. There are two car parks. Use the one nearest the village and take the path up to the waterfalls with the stream on your left at first, before crossing over to reach a well-maintained and broad path up to Aber Falls. As you approach the waterfall, go through a black gate and continue up to view the cascade before coming back and crossing the stream via the bridge. You are now also on the NWP (North Wales Path), so look

2 The path is easy to follow through gates and over streams and under powerlines as you eventually veer westerly, keeping to the contour of the hill at first with a slight uphill section as you pass under the powerlines again. Stunning views of Anglesey, Puffin Island, the Menai Straits, with the muttered roar of the A55 between you and the sea. A kissing gate takes you into fenced territory (with the fence on your left), and the path is easy to follow through an area newly resurfaced with stones, back under the

Aber Falls to Bangor

powerlines again to skirt woodland on your right, Nant Heilyn. Follow a good farm track as if towards a clump of pine trees, but keep them on your right down to a gate with a waymark in the corner. This takes you onto a lane and Bronydd Isaf. Turn LEFT.

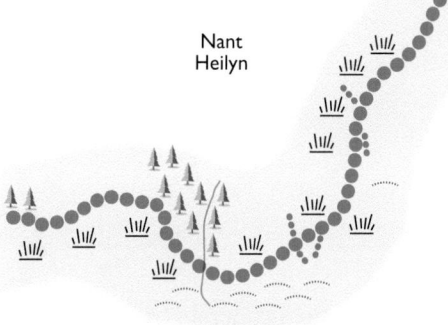

3 Follow the lane, ignoring another lane to the right, until you reach powerlines again and find a track off to the RIGHT marked Plâs-uchaf. You need to take two gates in and out of the farmyard to reach a field. Here the path divides, so go LEFT through a gate and in the next field strike broadly across as if towards woodland. You are joined by a wall on your right and the path eventually becomes a walled lane. It's easy to miss the next turning LEFT off the walled lane. At one point the lane broadens a little and the gate and path you need to find are tucked away on your left. Keep a lookout for this gate. Continue along this new direction now to a footbridge over a stream via slate steps to reach a road. Turn LEFT on the road and go uphill.

4 After a while you pass the entrance to Wern Bach, on your left, before finding a footpath signed NWP on the right where you can gain entrance into a field with a wall on your right. You now walk through redundant kissing gates with the building Pant-y-gwair on your right. Pass the gated entrance and continue through gorse and bramble in something of a scramble up by a stream. Keep this stream on your right to reach a metal ladder stile in the wall on your right, then over a low stone wall into a field with a fence on the right. A kissing gate in the corner of the field enables you to cross another field to a kissing gate and onto a lane. Turn RIGHT.

51

The Pilgrim's Way

5 Follow the lane. Pass under powerlines and at a track junction turn LEFT, going under powerlines again. You are now walking on a track towards Cochwillan.

Built in 1465 by William ap Gruffudd, ally of Henry Tudor on the battlefield at Bosworth, Cochwillan Old Hall is remarkably well-preserved, with hammerhead beam roof, screens and carvings of the period. Interior open only to visitors by appointment via the Penrhyn Estate, but exterior free to view by pilgrims passing by.

As you approach the building turn RIGHT (there is a waymark on a post) to pass in front of the house and then turn LEFT to skirt it again, through a gate between buildings. There is a kissing gate on the right, giving access into a field. A fence on the left guides you towards a wood, and at the end of this section turn RIGHT through a kissing gate into another field. Keep close to the left field edge. Take in a slate kissing gate, a field, another kissing gate and now you are approaching the river, Afon Ogwen, on your left, with a steep drop down. A kissing gate in the corner of the next field allows you to descend towards the river, keeping the hedge on your right. The final kissing gate takes you close to the former mill, Felin Cochwillan, where you can walk on the slate drive before turning LEFT towards the river. Go RIGHT to pass an outhouse and find a track towards the river which you cross by means of a green metal bridge. After the bridge go ahead to a kissing gate and a track.

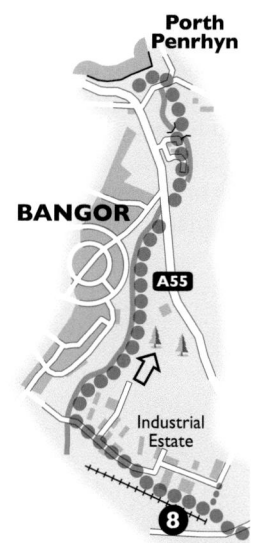

6 You join a concrete track and walk under the A55, climbing on similar concrete the other side to pass a different Welsh shrine, a rugby field, on your left. The path becomes a proper roadway after the rugby club, and at the road junction go LEFT, uphill. Look out for a clear waymark on a signpost taking you through bushes to a bus stop. Here you need to cross the busy road to find a kissing gate onto a path between hedge and fence. An airshaft on the right is a prominent feature. A kissing gate takes you onto a lane, which you cross. This is Llandygai on the map.

7 On the other side of the lane, cross the field with a small wood on your left hand side making for the industrial estate. Cross the track coming at you from right angles and continue between metal fences, with the railway line clearly visible down to your left until you reach a road, where you turn LEFT.

Aber Falls to Bangor

Penrhyn Quarry Railway. Left: steam railway bridge. Right: earlier horsedrawn railway bridge

8 Follow this road and continue downhill until you reach a barrier. Go round this obstacle and turn RIGHT onto the old railway line. This pleasant reclaimed walkway continues for some distance, passing under a white road bridge with artwork, until you reach a wooden bridge over a stream. You are now in Porth Penrhyn and reach the Cegin Viaduct. After passing underneath the bridge turn LEFT up to the A5. Cross this road and go down Penybryn Road, turning LEFT at the end to make your way into Bangor city centre.

The Penrhyn Quarry Railway was originally constructed in 1798, with the horse-drawn railway opening fully in 1801 as a means of transporting slate from Lord Penrhyn's quarries at Bethesda the 6 miles to the sea at Porth Penrhyn. By 1870 a longer route, powered by steam locomotives, continued until closure in 1962. Pilgrim's Way travellers follow two sections of the line here into Porth Penrhyn and then out again from Bangor on the way to Llanberis.

Bangor to Llanberis
11 miles

A varied walk takes you soon out of the cathedral city of Bangor along a former slate quarry railway line into open country before reaching the foot of Snowdon itself.

1 Walk up from the Cathedral and turn RIGHT into High Street, continuing past Capel Pendref followed by the Harp Inn on your left, to find a public footpath, LEFT, taking you up steps away from the town. Continue along this clear path with railings and a busy railway line down to the right and a wall on your left. As you go, ignore a downward path to the right and, continuing upwards, keep close to the high wall on your left. On the other side of the wall is a golf course, so look out for stray missiles coming your way! The path soon comes out onto a road. Turn LEFT here.

2 Walk along, on a pavement now, and at the road junction continue LEFT (waymark on a post), past the former hospital on your left until you run out of pavement. Descend now on the road, ignoring another road to the left. Views open out on both sides, the distinct shape of Penrhyn Castle over to the left, the Llanberis Pass ahead but more to your right. The road becomes steeper, and steeper still, until you take the next road off to your LEFT, which plunges down, under a bridge, to reach a ford at the bottom. Cross the river via a footbridge. Turn RIGHT onto the old quarry railway line to Tregarth, with a useful information board telling you about the Cegin Valley.

3 There follows a lengthy and pleasant stretch along the tarmac surface of a cycle path through trees close to the river (Afon Cegin) on your right. Gates take you in and out of a short stretch of genuine roadway, allowing you to pass underneath the snarling A55. Turn LEFT again and you are back onto the reclaimed cycleway, now gifted with a name, Lôn Ogwen. Walk on over the long walled bridge to reach a prominent new green bridge over the A4244, with glimpses of steam railway paraphernalia over to your left. This walkway takes you under first one bridge and then another, before going uphill to pass a house on the left and a tempting footpath, to be ignored, on your right. As you approach the next bridge, the main route dips down underneath it, but here you need to take the subsidiary path, LEFT, guiding you through a walkers' gate, where you turn RIGHT and cross over the bridge spanning the way you came.

4 Once over the bridge you need to look out for a subtle change of direction. You leave the path, which swings sharply round to the left, but

Bangor to Llanberis

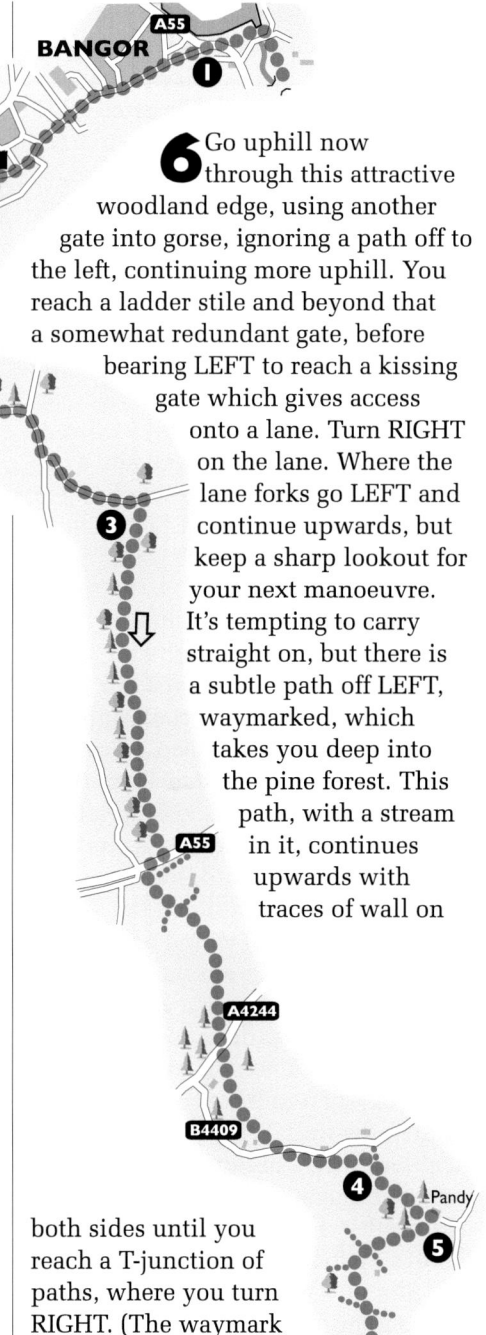

your route lies directly ahead. To do this, go through a walkers' gate, RIGHT, and immediately over a ladder stile, LEFT, which will take you into a field. Now continue on a track as it winds its way gradually up, with field edge and stream to your right. You pass interesting wooden buildings and a smallholding on your left, before turning RIGHT through an open gateway to reach inhabited buildings, Pandy, on your left, with a waymark. Turn RIGHT here, keeping an uninhabited building on your left, pass a small waterfall and go through a kissing gate, with a waymark on the post to your left, and into a field.

5 You need to follow a rough path keeping hawthorn and other trees on your left on a sort of low ridge with bluebells (in season). The countryside seems more open at this point, but make for woodland ahead, ignoring a path crossing the one you are on. Don't go uphill. There is a prominent wooden structure, which could have all sorts of uses, on your right, and a post in the ground labelled number 5 on your left, just before you plunge into woodland through a walker's gate. Follow the path for a short distance before finding a sturdy gate which gives access into managed woodland.

6 Go uphill now through this attractive woodland edge, using another gate into gorse, ignoring a path off to the left, continuing more uphill. You reach a ladder stile and beyond that a somewhat redundant gate, before bearing LEFT to reach a kissing gate which gives access onto a lane. Turn RIGHT on the lane. Where the lane forks go LEFT and continue upwards, but keep a sharp lookout for your next manoeuvre. It's tempting to carry straight on, but there is a subtle path off LEFT, waymarked, which takes you deep into the pine forest. This path, with a stream in it, continues upwards with traces of wall on both sides until you reach a T-junction of paths, where you turn RIGHT. (The waymark is on a tree)

55

7 Your path between gloomy pine trees is joined by a wall coming in from the left before you eventually reach a gate. Do not use the gate. Instead turn LEFT, through a gap in the wall. Once you have taken this turn, go upwards through mixed woodland to come out by way of a kissing gate. Continue along here, between a steep hillside with bilberries coming down on your left and a wall on your right, until your path opens out. Views of the coastline emerge now on your right, as the stony path takes you under power lines to reach a gate in a wall and a good stop for your packed lunch. Go through the gate, turning LEFT in the walled lane.

8 Go uphill to reach the house, Tynllidiart, and immediately descend along a metalled road to the RIGHT, with good views continuing over on your right. But keep a sharp look out for a footpath, and signpost, on your LEFT through a kissing gate to follow a farm track towards Cae'r-gôf. Pass these farm buildings on your right and continue ahead on the level (waymark on a post) to find a rough cart track taking you out into more open country. You reach a gate and a kissing gate, rather detached, in the wall to the LEFT, to pick up this rough cart track again as it continues through a gap in the wall. Where paths diverge go ahead, with a building to the left, and on through another gap in a wall and another. However, after this wall there is a subtle change of direction.

9 Go uphill here, half LEFT to an exit point which you can't see. As you climb further uphill a waymark on a post appears plus a hidden gate in the wall ahead, hidden, because it's sideways on and you may not see it before you reach it! Turn RIGHT here onto common land. Continue now with the wall on your right, gradually descending, realising you seem to be making a detour, which in fact you are. In the next field corner there is a walkers' gate. Go through here into quite different territory. You face rough and boggy terrain as you descend half LEFT. I imagine this section would be hard work in wet weather and difficult to navigate in mist. There are marker posts (one uprooted) which help you maintain a direct line to reach a gully, a stream, a wall and trees. This is one of those occasions when you will know you have arrived when you reach it, but it may be baffling to find in difficult circumstances!

10 Once up from the gully, for a while skirt round the hill which is over to your left. More posts keep you close to the wall on your right through a broken wall to reach another marker post urging you to change direction, LEFT. Here you go sternly uphill, aiming for the deserted ruin. Go to the right of the ruin and immediately turn LEFT, through a gate, keeping the wall on your left for a short distance before following the path more uphill, striking across moorland. The terrain changes again, as you walk through heather, bilberries and bracken, hill-walking now, aiming as if for a prominent high ridge in the distance. Keep following the distinctive, wayward path upwards.

Bangor to Llanberis

As you reach the crest, the magnificent peak of Snowdon appears ahead, seen from an untypical viewpoint but unmistakeable, if the weather is kind.

11 Soon you reach a kissing gate in a wall and begin the descent, keeping close to the wall on your right to find another hidden sideways gate in the field corner. In this next field keep the wall to your right and continue downhill between two low walls to reach a wooden gate which takes you suddenly out of the countryside and into the back yard of a house, Ffridd uchaf. Keep this house to your right and look out for a way leading off the drive, RIGHT, to follow a secluded path (with a waymark) to reach a kissing gate providing access onto a main road where you turn RIGHT.

12 Continue along this main road, looking out for the second footpath off to the LEFT through a kissing gate and onto a bridle path, taking you towards habitation, another kissing gate and a rapid descent into the village of Deiniolen, where you turn LEFT onto High Street. Almost immediately (past the Bull public house) you turn RIGHT into New Street, passing a shop on the right where you can top up supplies before turning LEFT into a street, Tai Caradog. Continue along this street, turning RIGHT at the end through a kissing gate, descending to reach two footbridges over a stream, before going up again to reach a kissing gate onto a lane where you turn LEFT at Garnedd. Almost at once turn RIGHT off the lane, to find a footpath and a kissing gate which gives access onto rough land with an uneven surface. The only way now is up. At the fork, the path narrows and climbs between walls to reach a house. Go through the gate here and continue upwards along the driveway to the road, where you turn LEFT.

13 Follow the road for a while, going RIGHT where it joins another road. You reach houses on the left, Maes Eilian, and a bus shelter appears on your right. Llanberis Lake is now very prominent, over to the right, and you may be tempted to think you are almost at your destination. Then you realise Llanberis is on the far side

57

The Pilgrim's Way

Llyn Llanberis

of the lake! Just before the bus shelter there is a kissing gate and footpath descending, with steps, and this is your route. Go down to a lane, cross it and find another footpath opposite, between buildings, turning RIGHT just beyond, onto an access road. As this road takes a sharp turn to the right, go LEFT instead, through a gate and into woodland. There follows a pleasant walk over a metal bridge and via a kissing gate through into Padarn Country Park. A long descent follows through woodland and slate, slippery underfoot at times, as you make your way downwards along the many paths to the old hospital and the Quarry Museum at the foot. You may have time to visit the Quarry Museum (*though it closes at 1700*) before taking a short cut to Llanberis itself, just turning RIGHT before the main road. *The National Slate Museum at Glifach Ddu is constructed out of the 19th*

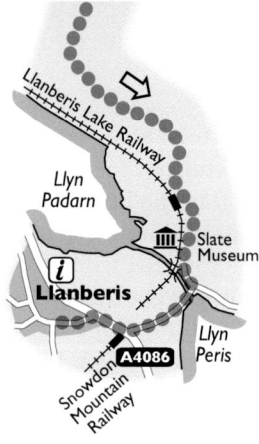

century workshops of the now defunct Dinorwig quarry which opened in 1787 and closed in 1969. Nearby is the Hospital, a grim reminder of the cost to human life and well-being, while mounds of slate lie all around you, themselves a shrine to a lost and mighty industry and the families of the men who worked and died there.

Llanberis to Penygroes
12 miles

Bracing hill-walking over the foothills of Snowdonia. There are trains too, but not the way you need to go.

1 Leave the main street in Llanberis by way of Capel Coch Road, signposted to the Youth Hostel. Soon after passing the impressive chapel on your left take the road to the RIGHT and go uphill. Almost on the brow of the hill ignore the road to the right and continue ahead, shortly changing direction LEFT into a road marked Plas Garnedd and follow this road steeply uphill to reach an old gate across the road. You may hear the sound of Snowdon's railway engines over to your left, clattering away, and catch sight even of smoke from the trains. There are good views too as you look back at Llanberis. Go through the gateway you've reached and continue upwards until you come to a sharp right-hand bend in the road, with a deserted building on the left. Soon the tarmac ends. Follow the road, a track now, up to a gate which marks the end of the roadway, and use the ladder stile to gain access onto more open country. You are now at the foot of the highest mountain in England and Wales, *Snowdon rises to 3560 feet above sea level. If you want to climb up while you are here, the path from Llanberis is probably the easiest, though least interesting route. The Mountain Railway, a narrow gauge rack and pinion railway also takes passengers on the 4¾ mile journey to the top.*

2 Pick out a track on your LEFT which follows a wall, and keeping the wall to your left climb on uphill. On the brow of the hill you will see disused quarries and a lake to your right before you go through a gate and pass a notice banning vehicles. Keeping the wall to your right you will eventually reach the top of the climb, Ty'n-y-mynydd. Go through a gate and then begin the downhill stretch through a kissing gate, descending to a forest plantation on your left. After the plantation the road becomes metalled again and you follow this downhill, looking out for a well-marked footpath on your LEFT to Hafod Oleu, waymarked with a dragonfly. Go through the kissing gate. Leave the road now and continue along the track, past two white single-story cottages. Cross what could be a ford in wet weather, though a dry pathway over a stream bed in our case, and go through a gate. Now turn RIGHT for the descent via several typically small fields.

3 The path is distinct and easy to follow, with many waymarks, first with the [dry] stream to your right. Pass under power lines and turn RIGHT. There is a subtle change of direction, RIGHT, well signposted, although a broken gate proved to be

The Pilgrim's Way

an obstacle on our walk. Follow the wall and the path down through a host of small fields, with horses. As you reach habitation, Bryn y Pistyll you cross a hidden access road, so look out for vehicles. By the way that *is* a train you may hear, hooting in the distant countryside – as you approach the Welsh Highland Railway. At the end of the descent, turn RIGHT along a track which becomes a road and continue until you reach the main road, where you turn LEFT. You have reached Waunfawr.

4 Carry on walking along the main road and cross the river via the bridge. Traffic is kettled into one lane, so look out for rampaging vehicles. After the river comes another bridge over the bijou railway line and following that the Snowdonia Parc Inn, with its wide range of facilities including camping. You may want to stop for a pint, but there is a steep climb and 7 miles walking ahead! Carry on along the main road and look out for a road off to the RIGHT, signposted Rhosgadfan. The road is narrow and traffic can still be busy. You will soon reach a footpath off to the LEFT with a large sign telling you this is the way to Y Fron, so leave the road by way of the ladder stile and start the fairly steep climb upwards through bracken, in season. Use orange arrows on rocks as a guide over what has been described as a stream, although in dry summers there is little water. As you wind your way upwards through woodland, Parc Dudley, you reach a metal ladder stile (it's loose, beware) over a wall. The path continues to pick its way uphill. As you stop for a breather, look back for your last long gaze at Snowdon directly behind you. You come to a second metal ladder stile over a wall (this one is secure), and afterwards push up beyond the tree line, making for 'The Common'.

5 A stile in a field corner, with wooden steps and a waymark, takes you into more open territory, initially through a gap between tall stone walls into an abandoned smallholding Ty'n-y-Graig. Come out

Llanberis to Penygroes

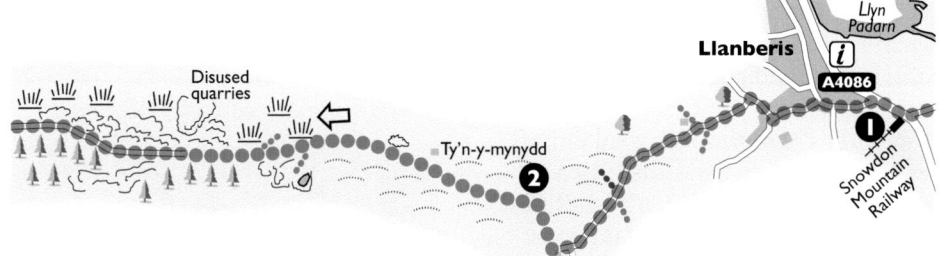

at the top boundary by means of a gate. You are now in open country. Navigating could be tricky here in mist or bad weather. If you can see clearly, aim to walk upwards, leftish, as if towards some point on the horizon where the slopes of two distant hillsides appear to meet. In the first instance make for a spot somewhat to the LEFT part of the wall ahead. If you cannot see well, just carry on walking upwards until you reach the wall facing you, turn LEFT and continue, keeping the wall on your right until you reach the end of it. It is in fact the corner of a wall. There is a low level waymark on a post here, which will confirm you are on track. Turn the corner, still keeping the wall on your right. Now the path gradually leaves the wall, moving away to the LEFT, its surface littered with grey and white stones, a useful navigational aid, but uneven underfoot. You are now walking more on the level, in terms of gradient. The next landmark is the projecting wall corner of a cottage boundary on your right. Keep the cottage on your right and then go downhill a touch to reach a track which you follow, now turning LEFT and away from the cottage. This section could be quite difficult to navigate in bad weather.

6 Walk along the track from the cottage, heading for the next property Hafod Ruffydd, which is approached by a sort of concrete ramp. Pass the house on your right and pick up the metalled road which leaves it. As the road turns sharp right, with its little wayside garden, you need to pick up the footpath which goes sharply off to the LEFT at right angles. Do not go up the track ahead. The footpath is more discreet, and winds its way through heather, with several waymarks on posts. Views are glorious, particularly of the spectacular Nantlle Ridge gradually emerging on your left hand side. Also, down to the left, is a fir plantation, and up on your right the brooding shapes of waste tips from old slate workings. Your path continues in and out of the heather until you come to a very distinctive large rock on your right-hand side, just off the track. Change direction and pass close to this rock, keeping it on your right and continue uphill, the waste tips becoming more distinctive. You are toiling upwards still, and into a headwind maybe, but eventually the path gives itself a bit of a shake and you now find yourself actually walking into the quarry, Bryn Fferan. This is now being worked by a local farmer,

The Pilgrim's Way

converting tons of waste slate into various grades of crushed material for ornamental and gravel use.

7 Follow the approach road out of the quarry as far as the (filled in) cattle grid. Here take a footpath RIGHT towards a house, passing it on your right and then veer towards another house, leftish, with a waymark on a

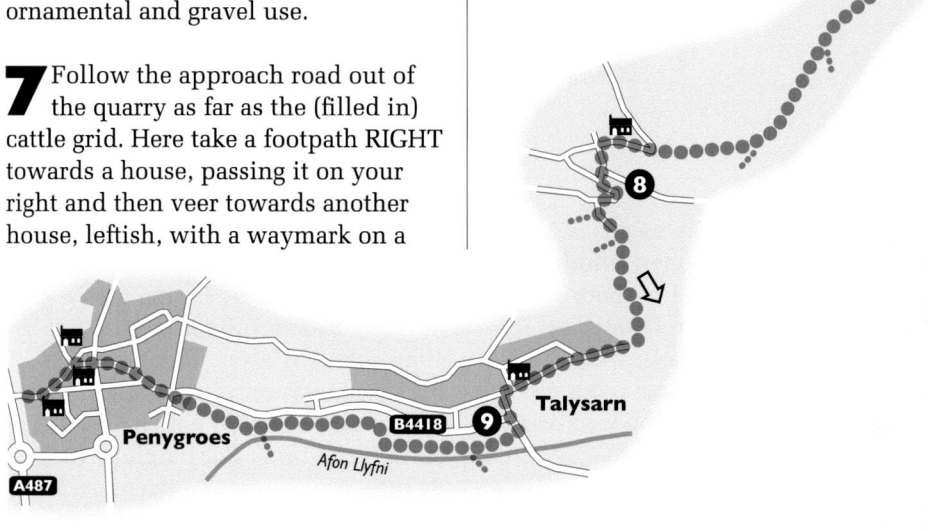

post in the corner of the wall. Keeping the house to your left, navigate your way round a perilously deep hole, on your right, its dark waters looming dank and forbidding. You reach a somewhat wide expanse of open ground which is in fact the substance of a cross roads. You are now at Y Fron. Continue in the direction you have been following, cross the road and pick up a track making towards a row of cottages, with the sign Tai Bryn Twrog. Another good navigational target is the slim radio mast on the horizon. The tarmac of this road turns to stone after you have passed the row of cottages along the old slate tramway. The track is now walled on both sides, and an interesting placard on your left gives you some fascinating history of the area. Pass houses to right and left before reaching a junction, with a converted chapel ahead, in the crook of two paths. If you want to look for the shrine here, go as if towards the old red phone box and in the chapel wall opposite, there is the somewhat imprisoned fibreglass statue of St Theresa of the Roses (St Thérèse of Lisieux). Apparently she is the patron saint of suffering, so this might be a good moment to call on her, if your feet are sore after the long walk. However, pressing on, go LEFT at the chapel junction, picking up a track which takes you down to a recently abandoned quarry, its gates firmly shut.

8 As you approach the locked gates there is a cunning tunnel to the RIGHT of the approach road which you use to continue your journey. The path now falls downhill through a kissing gate and narrow pathways, sharp slate and stones underfoot at times, at first with a wall to your right. This path then goes between two walls,

Clynnog Fawr church

through more kissing gates, down stone steps to a gate on your RIGHT. Leave the downward plunge now and use the gate to gain access through to a track where you turn LEFT, continuing downhill to reach the end of the descent. Turn RIGHT along a track which becomes a metalled lane and proceed towards a roundabout with trees on it. You are now in Talysarn. Walk LEFT here down a broad lane and go through a kissing gate on your LEFT then turn RIGHT. There are two distinct hard-surface paths facing you, so take the RIGHT hand one which brings you to a football pitch on your left, and continue along the pathway until another kissing gate takes you out onto a road.

9 At the road you find yourself at a junction, so turn LEFT and cross the road onto the only pavement opposite and follow it downhill. Look out for a sign on the RIGHT just after the 50mph sign, and follow the footpath indicated, to plunge into undergrowth along by the river. Follow this waterside path, but when you reach a footbridge over the river do not take it, and continue, instead, along by the river, Afon Llyfni. The last time I was here the path was overgrown, and deceptive hollows and stones lie beneath. Go through two kissing gates. After the second kissing gate the path swings away from the river to gain a raised slate causeway, eventually bringing you to a kissing gate with access onto the main road (B4418) where you turn LEFT. There is a good footpath on the other side of the busy road which will take you into Penygroes.

The Pilgrim's Way

Penygroes to Trefor
10½ miles

Through a quiet, pastoral landscape continue your quest for St Bueno's church and well at Clynnog Fawr and reach the coast of the spectacular Llŷn peninsula.

1 From the crossroads in the centre of Penygroes go down Snowdon Street, which becomes Market Place, turns into Station Road, finally deciding to become Clynnog Road, where houses end. In front of you is the footbridge over the A487. Cross the footbridge and turn RIGHT, picking up the tarmac cycle path which runs parallel to the main road. Look out for a sudden footpath waymarked on the LEFT and go through a gate into the field. After about 50 yards ignore a tempting footpath to the left and continue ahead, with a low wall to your left and the open field to your right. Go through a red field gate. With the wall on your left now slightly higher, forge ahead to the field corner, where there is a waymark. Pass through a slate-shielded kissing gate here and continue ahead

through a field with gorse, step across a ground-level wooden footbridge, and make for a gap in a stone wall. This takes you into a field with bracken. Passing through another gap in a stone wall, approach a kissing gate and go into a field. Make for the left-hand field corner ahead to a track and cattle grid which you cross. Follow the track and leave the fields behind you for a while.

2 Ignore the left turn to Minffordd and continue to the end of the track to reach a T-junction where you turn LEFT. You reach a crossroad of lanes. Go straight across, following the lane to Pant Eithinog. Pass this farmhouse and continue along the track past another, Eithinog Uchaf, with glimpses of the sea and high

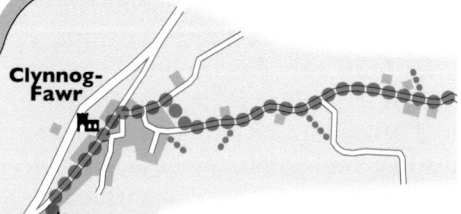

ground on Anglesey over to your right. Continuing along the track into a field you find yourself on a raised grassy ridge. Make for the building over to your LEFT, Eithinog Ganol, and use the gate in the field

Penygroes to Tefor

to gain access onto a lane by the side of the house. Keep the house on your right and continue down the lane to join a tarmac road. Turn LEFT.

3 After a short distance turn RIGHT onto a farm track, with a waymark, to Glan Rafon Bach, passing the house with its monkey puzzle tree on your right. Go down to the river, crossing Afon Llyfni by a footbridge to enter what can best be described as a glade. Leave the glade through an old gateway, with stone pillars to each side, turning RIGHT

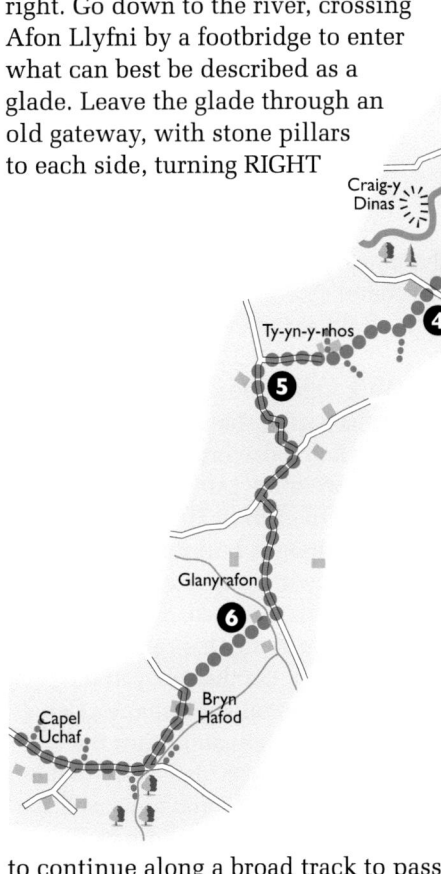

to continue along a broad track to pass through first a gate and then a kissing gate to reach an access track to Lleuar Fawr. Go between the farmhouse on your right and farm buildings on your left, continuing straight ahead along field edges with gates across to

reach the approach to Lleuar Fach/Bach. Turn RIGHT as if towards the farmhouse, but just in front of the gate there is a small gate, LEFT, which helps you skirt the property, keeping the barn on your right. At the edge of the barn cross into the field over a fence/closed gate.

4 The next section is rather obscure and the path does not seem to agree with the description given in the official route nor tally with the pathways on the OS map, as I understand it. This seems to be the best description of the way to go: once in the field, after the barn at Lleuar Bach, your general line of direction is to make for a house (Ty-yn-y-rhos) in the same direction you have been travelling. So cross the field, passing under overhead power lines, a useful

65

The Pilgrim's Way

guide, to reach a field gate. Go through this gate and continue ahead, with the field edge on your right to pass through another field gate. The property you have been aiming for now appears

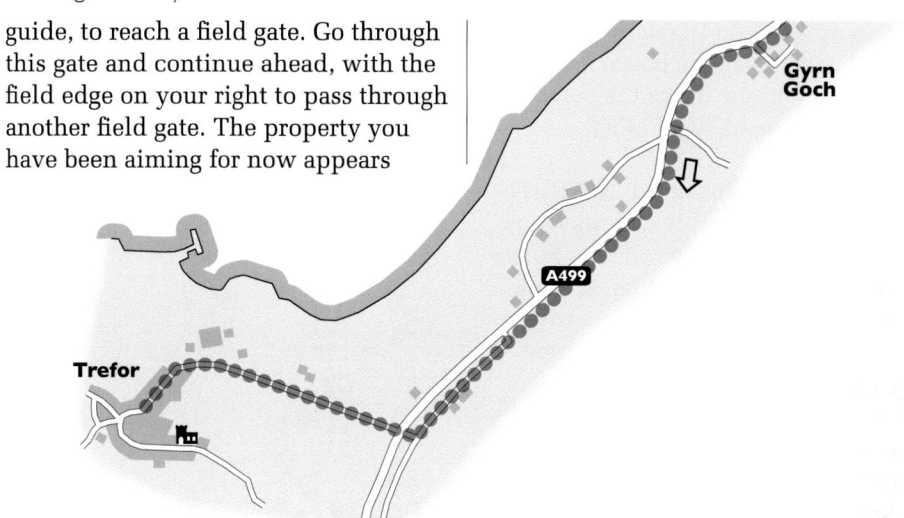

closer, over to the right, and as you continue you will pass the house, Ty-yn-yrhos, which is close by, over the hedge to your right. Now follow a relatively new hedgerow on your right. Not far along there is a gate, RIGHT, in the hedgerow and you can go through here to reach the access track to the house. Turn LEFT and follow the track away from the house. Navigation is now easier. Continue along the track to reach a road. Turn LEFT.

5 Follow this road for a short distance and turn RIGHT at the T-junction. Continue along the road looking for another road off to the LEFT, which goes up hill. Take this road, first up then downhill. Now look out for an access road, RIGHT, which will take you down to houses and a river. It has the odd title of Restricted Byway. At the bottom you come to a ford over the river with a handy footbridge to the left of the ford. Cross the bridge and as you approach the house at Glanyrafon go LEFT to a wooden gate, which will bring you into a field at the foot of a hill.

6 Walk uphill, not severe, but probably the steepest of the day, with the field edge on your left. Go through two more gates and approach the farmyard of Bryn Hafod, where you pass between buildings to reach a lane taking you away from the house. When you come to a road, turn RIGHT and continue along this road towards Clynnog Fawr. On the rise you pass the site of a demolished chapel, Capel Uchaf, on your left, and begin the descent towards the historic settlement of Clynnog Fawr. As you approach the village, look out for a cunning tarmac footpath, off to your LEFT, which takes you directly into the village close to the church, a must-see building, dedicated to Saint Bueno. The large, sparsely decorated Church is one of those centres where you can stamp your 'passport'. Once you have looked

The beach at Nefyn

round the church, come back to the road, turn RIGHT and walk out of the village along the road, the 'old' road as it is called, now that the village has the luxury of a new road. Just outside the village, on your left, easily missed, is St Bueno's well, Ffynnon Bueno. *Though St Bueno founded the church and well in the 7th century, the extensive existing buildings are late 15th/early 16th century. Artefacts include a medieval chest, choir stalls and screen, and outside a 10th century sundial. On the Pilgrim's Way, as you leave the village, look out for St Bueno's well [Ffynnon Bueno], a spring flowing into a square stone pool with stepped seats on two sides.*

7 The Pilgrim's Way now follows the old road, which is often very close to the new road, for two and a half miles of tedious tarmac before you reach a welcome sign taking you perilously over the A499 to a road into the settlement of Trefor and the Irish Sea, your constant companion now to the end of the Pilgrim's Way.

The Pilgrim's Way

Trefor to Towyn

14 miles (this section of the route can be taken in two halves, with a break at Nefyn)

After the steep climb up from Trefor, you will be rewarded with wonderful views of the Llŷn peninsula ahead, before you follow the spectacular coastline.

Note *that there are alternative routes on these later sections, using the coastal path. The directions that follow are for the official 'more inland' routes.*

1 Start in the centre of Trefor at a junction of several roads. With your back to the useful shop, cross over the 'main' road and take a curiously unnamed street facing you. Cross over a bridge, pass the chapel on your right and the car park on your left, which you may want to use anyway for the start of today's walk. As the houses end, turn LEFT up a tarmac lane, and begin your steady climb up to Bwlch yr Eifl. This is the most severe climb of the day, and a long one. You may want to stop occasionally for a breather and look back at the fantastic views of the coastline behind.

2 Continue up the lane, ignoring the footpath coming in from the right, which is in fact the longer coastal route joining in. There is a waymark here. Continue upwards, the theme for this section of the walk, passing through a

new black gate as gradually the lane becomes a track and before long a path. At a junction of paths, go upwards, with a ruined house on your right, through a stone pillared gateway to a walkers' gate with waymark. As you climb upwards, the path is flanked by a fence on your right, and a line of electricity poles coming in from the left. These features could be useful markers in mist or low cloud, which happened to us on the day we climbed. And it is a climb. Free-ranging goats loom (or are they sheep with horns? – hard to distinguish in the mist). You now pass under the same electricity poles while the fence on your right projects into your path. A difficult piece of navigation follows here if visibility is poor. You need to leave this projecting fence corner (and its waymark) and climb half RIGHT into open territory, with the path more obscure. You are making for another

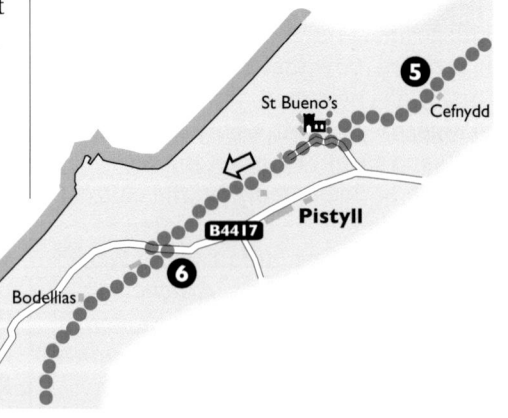

Tefor to Towyn

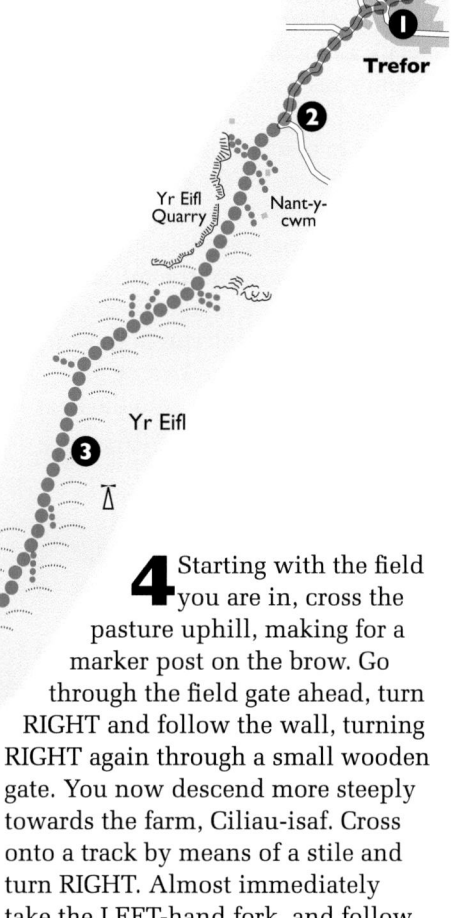

fence corner, which you may be able to see as you climb. At this point there is a waymark, but not a Pilgrim's Way one. You are now almost on the shoulder of the Bwlch and reach a track coming from the disused quarries to your right. Turn LEFT and follow the track. You are finally at the top.

3 The descent is much easier, it's downhill after all, and the track is broad and clear. If it's still misty, beware of at least one point where part of the track has slipped down the mountainside to your right, otherwise this is a good chance to stride out to the car park ahead. Down to the right you can see the Welsh Language Centre, Nant Gwrtheyrn, by the sea, and in the distance the long stretch of coastline of the majestic Llŷn peninsula. A truly exhilarating walk if the weather is on your side. At the car park at Mount Pleasant turn LEFT along the metalled road for a short distance, before leaving it to follow a bridle path on your RIGHT through a metal gate, keeping the ditch and fence to your right and the house, Tir Gwyn, to your left. Take the next gate to the RIGHT and go into the field. You now follow quite a long section of field and gate territory, not always clear on the ground, and often inhabited by livestock.

4 Starting with the field you are in, cross the pasture uphill, making for a marker post on the brow. Go through the field gate ahead, turn RIGHT and follow the wall, turning RIGHT again through a small wooden gate. You now descend more steeply towards the farm, Ciliau-isaf. Cross onto a track by means of a stile and turn RIGHT. Almost immediately take the LEFT-hand fork, and follow this for a short distance. You seem to be walking away from the farm, but suddenly a waymarked path makes you almost double up on yourself, and you now continue between fences to reach a stile. You are back on track, passing to the left of the farm, Ciliau-isaf. After the kissing-gate turn RIGHT, as if into the farm itself, but then use a ladder stile, LEFT, and find another kissing gate which will take you, via steps, onto a sunken path leading from the house. This manoeuvre has

The Pilgrim's Way

in fact simply taken you round the property which you now leave behind to walk along the track. You are now in somewhat more featureless field territory. Follow the line of fence on the right to reach a kissing-gate. Now aim for a fence, on the skyline, which seems to jut out. Using the power lines coming in from the left as a marker, you reach the brow of the hill and need to make for a rather distant field boundary. Follow the run of power lines until you see the kissing gate which gives you access into the next field, surrounded perhaps by rollicking bullocks. Keep the fence line on your left in the next field and reach another kissing gate taking you out of this field into another. Walking downhill towards the farm, Cefnydd, the path becomes more conspicuous.

5 From Cefnydd the path eventually winds its way down to a lane. Turn RIGHT here to visit the fascinating 15th century St Bueno's church, tucked away in the hillside, its floor carpeted with rushes.

Pilgrims can visit another church founded by St Bueno, at Pistyll. Current buildings are 15th century, some 12th century. The roof, now slated, was thatched until modern times. The interior is noted for floor coverings of herbs and rushes, wall-painting and an 11th century font.

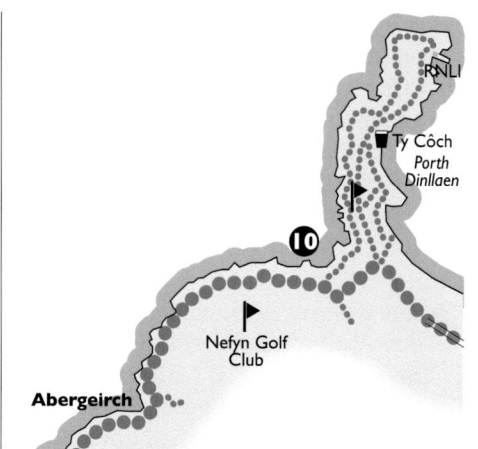

Coming out of the church, retrace your steps back to the lane and turn RIGHT to join the well-marked Wales Coast Path as you skirt the inhabited areas around Pistyll. The path can be followed easily enough through gates and small fields, past the edge of a camp site, as you make your way towards the main road, the B4417. There was just one point where the waymarking seemed ambiguous, as you reach a projecting fence corner and need to walk more steeply up to your LEFT than the waymark suggests. However it's really plain sailing to the road, and once there turn LEFT.

6 Walk along the road for a short distance and take the track off to your RIGHT, signed Ty Mawr, and continue along a well-marked path to Nefyn. The path hugs the hillside to your left, passing numerous occasional dwellings (Bodellias), once even crossing someone's front lawn it

Tefor to Towyn

seems, but all well-signed. The path eventually narrows and you take a right-hand turn to reach a small stream on your right. In this small field, or paddock, you are quite close to the

and broad sands invite you. You reach a slipway and descend down to beach level, so you can have your dip after all, if there's time, otherwise climb up

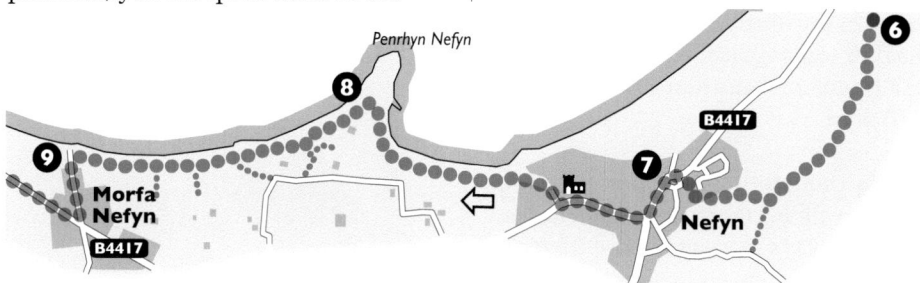

church and need to find a gate in the right-hand corner to take you out, bearing LEFT round the church and through another passageway into the small town of Nefyn.

7 Leave the centre of Nefyn by tracing the main road up as far as the crossroads, where you turn RIGHT to follow the main road, Pen-y-Bryn which goes to Aberdaron. After you have passed St David's church on the right look out for the road off to the RIGHT called Lon y Traeth which will take you down to the beach. Before you descend sharply, as if to the shore, keep to a walkers' path on the LEFT which will bring you onto the cliff top walk. Once again the Pilgrim's Way joins forces with the Wales Coast Path and is well-marked throughout.

8 First of all the cliff top path rounds the headland of Penrhyn Nefyn before continuing along a path, narrow at times, almost channelled out of the earth, taking you towards the projecting promontory of Porth Dinllaen. Over to your right the sea

the other side and find yourself in a busy car park at Morfa Nefyn.

9 Once in the car park go LEFT to find the road and turn RIGHT here, following the road up to the golf club. When you reach these premises go through a kissing gate to the RIGHT of the barrier and you are now in quite unusual territory for a rambler: a golf course. That's right, a golf course. So carry on down the road in front of you to the maintenance shed on the left-hand side, where you will actually venture out onto the hallowed turf itself, ill-equipped as you are for a round of golf. You can take an interesting diversion around the headland here, coming back to this point. You *have* to cross the fairway, but there is little official guidance on the ground, so be bold. Turn sharp LEFT at the maintenance shed and walk straight across the fairway. First of all there is a dip and what looks like a waymark, which turns out to be a golfers' distance marker. From here carry on uphill towards the bushes

71

The Pilgrim's Way

and there you will find a walkers' marker, steering you sharply RIGHT as if towards the sea. At this point you have to cross the pathway of driving golfers, so keep a sharp lookout for missiles (seriously!) until you come to the cliff top path again, where you turn LEFT and continue along on your way to Towyn.

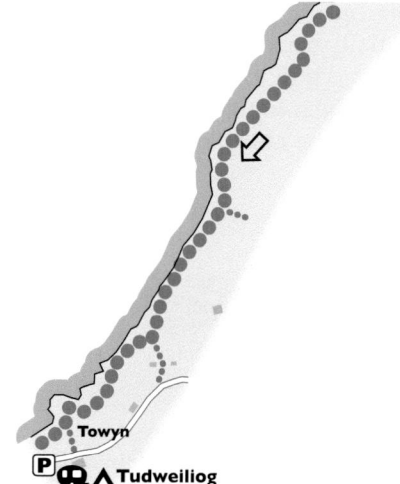

10 There follows a superb cliff top walk for more than three miles, the sea always close at hand with sight of oyster catchers and cormorants and even the occasional seal, while the grass is filled with harebells and meadowsweet and one or two orchids even. The golf course comes to an end, (check your score) and you descend somewhat precipitously, to the pipeline at Abergeirch, crossing via a footbridge to climb up the other side. There are three or four similar crossings of creeks and gullies as you walk exhilarated along by the sea. Gradually the caravans of Towyn come into view and your day's walk is near an end. Towyn turns out not to be a village as much as a house and a collection of caravans. To reach the nearest inhabited spot, leave the house on your left and continue up through three fields to the village of Tudweiliog. Here there is a post office, *which closes at 17.00*, if you want your passport stamped. The friendly Lion Hotel which serves food and drink all day, is just down the road and is highly recommended. There is also a bus which we caught to take us back to Trefor, *leaving at 1745, but check current times.*

Looking back at Yr Eifl from Nefyn

Towyn to Aberdaron
11½ miles

An exhilarating walk along the coastal path, breaking off inland across fields to reach Aberdaron as you complete the land section of your pilgrimage.

1 There is a car park at the caravan complex at Towyn, just along the track away from the shop, a useful place to start if you are planning a day's walk to Aberdaron. Getting back to base is slightly more complicated. We caught the Pwhelli bus from Aberdaron as far as Sarn Meyllteyrn and a taxi from there to Towyn.

2 Leave the car park and return to the house 'Towyn' before going down via the caravan site to rejoin the Coastal Path, but ignore the sign down to the beach itself unless you want to paddle in the sea before starting the walk. Instead turn LEFT and keep to the higher ground past the prominent bench, a good marker. The Coastal Path is generally easy to follow, well-marked, typically with a good, stout (new) fence on your left with agricultural land beyond, and new galvanised self-closing gates and kissing gates along the route. After the bench go through the first of these many kissing gates and cross a footbridge over a stream to reach another caravan site. A feature of the coastal path are the numerous streams coming in from the left, or creeks pushing in from the sea, at times involving considerable detours inland. Not in this case, as the first stream is easily crossed. Go through the caravan site and use the waymarker to follow a path through a gate to reach that typical onward path, slippery and eroded by sheep into something more like a channel, with fence and occasional earth embankment on your

73

The Pilgrim's Way

left. The sea is rolling in, alive with cormorants and oystercatchers, as you continue to follow the coastline.

3 You pass through a redundant gate and climb occasional steps up onto the embankment. You may notice a trig point, 20m above sea level as you make for what seems to be a deserted building on the edge of the coast which turns out to be no more than a solitary gable end. Turn LEFT before you reach it and instead arrive at Porth Ysgaden, which is itself no more than a single old building, although it has an interesting well, or perhaps a limekiln, now unfortunately a repository for rubbish. Cross a track to a kissing gate with a Pilgrim's Way sign joining the waymark signage and a signpost telling you the beach at Traeth Penllech is 2 miles away, so go for it. You pass another cove, Porth Gwylan, and eventually reach yet another, Porth Ychain to carry on along the coast. The pathway above the inlet at Penrhyn Melyn is liable to crumble, so extra care on this narrow section is needed. This is also the case before making a slippery descent down the cliff to sea level, at Traeth Penllech. Here you cross a stile and find yourself on the beach. The coastal path continues up and over to the left, but if it's low tide you can walk along the beach, pass a protruding buttress-like stone before regaining the cliff top again through a new black gate. This beach walk is not recommended at high tide as the beach will not be available!

Towyn to Aberdaron

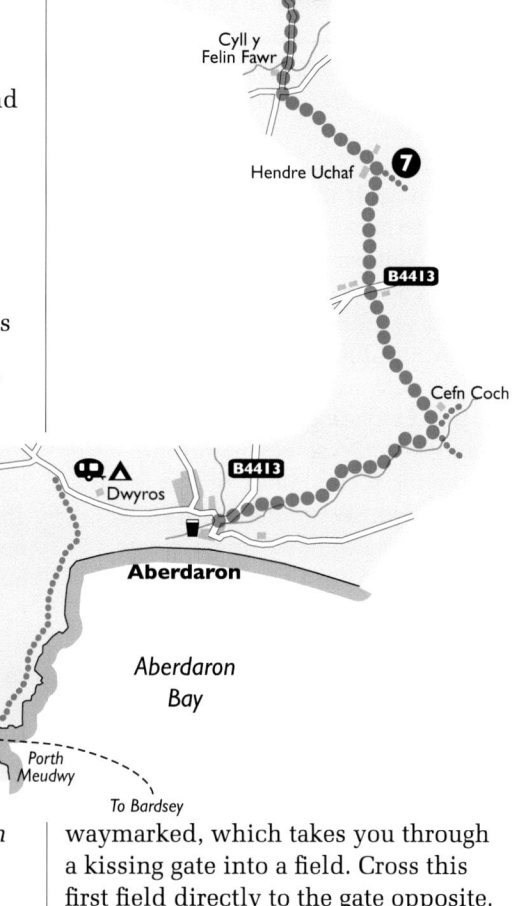

4 Your next target is Porth Colmon, with more traces of human habitation before you continue to Porth Widlin. At this point care is needed to keep to the coastal path and not get swept inland on the former path. The coastal path has now been recently improved to follow the coastline from Porth Widlin all the way to Whistling Sands. The newly opened section includes a close visit to the delightful beach of Port Iago, as the path winds in and out along the cliff, making the prospect of a cup of tea at Whistling Sands as far away as ever. You eventually go down to the beach and can walk along the sand, which allegedly makes a noise as you cross over, although the earth did not move for me. At the far end of the beach find the café, formerly the 'Coal Hole Café', with extensive facilities, outside tables, cups of tea and barra brith, *open every day in high summer and closing at 1800.*

5 Here the Pilgrim's Way leaves the Coastal Path and takes a more involved route inland, apparently shorter, but involving a considerable amount of field and gate work. Walk up from the Coal Hole Café along the tarmac access road to reach another road at a T junction where you turn RIGHT. After the road bends look out for a waymarked track, LEFT, mostly concreted, not kind to the feet. When this access road turns sharply left, look out for a path on your RIGHT, waymarked, which takes you through a kissing gate into a field. Cross this first field directly to the gate opposite. Cross the second field to the gate opposite. After this gate, the third in a row, the path turns sharp LEFT as you cross the field via a kissing gate. In the fourth field you are keeping the house and garden and fence to your left. Follow the fence to find a gate in the field corner. A second kissing gate follows almost immediately and you are now in a large field. Aim for the small gate ahead just to the right of the electricity pole, cross the field and go through the gate. Another large field

The Pilgrim's Way

appears. Once again aim for a grey gate ahead which appears to be just to the right of electricity poles ahead. Cross this field to reach a kissing gate which takes you out onto a lane, where you turn RIGHT.

6 With fields now behind you, follow the tarmac lane and a change of terrain. You pass houses and come to a crossroads of sorts. Go ahead. Just past the junction you will find a path off to your LEFT via a kissing gate and you are back into fields again. Cross the first field straight across to a grey kissing gate. Go somewhat uphill now in the second field, with a fence to your right. When the fence ends you need to negotiate a path across the field in front of you, and this may be difficult in wet or misty weather. You pass under power lines, walking uphill, rightish. Aim for the projecting field edge which comes in from the left and a marker post with a white top. Now keep this fence and gorse close on your left to reach a field corner. Go through two walkers' gates here, close together, before negotiating a straight pathway across the (third) field in front of you. Aim for a point just to the right of the farmhouse, Hendre-uchaf, and go to a gate in the field boundary between the house and the barn. Go through the gate, with a bird box on the left, and a waymark, and continue between farm and barn to reach the access track where you turn RIGHT.

7 Follow the access track upwards, over the cattle grid, until you begin to see Bardsey Island (at last!) over to the right, as it looms in the distance like a hump-backed whale, while ahead lie the two islands of Ynys Gwylan Fawr and Ynys Gwylan Bach, off the coast beyond Aberdaron Bay. Go over another cattle grid and you will reach the B 4413 road. Cross over the road and pick up the access track opposite. Continue along this track until you reach the gate across the track, which is the boundary of Cefn Coch. Go through the kissing gate, RIGHT, into a field and a possible reception committee of bullocks. Turn LEFT in this field and follow the line of the fence on your left, but not close to it. In fact you move gradually to the right, away from the hedge, aiming for an outbreak of thorn bushes. Eventually you will see and reach a marker post to the left of a distinctive hawthorn bush, described in the official guide as 'wind-affected', which it certainly is. Plunge down the steep gully ahead making for the river. After a kissing gate you will reach a footbridge over the river which you do not use. Instead turn RIGHT to follow a path along by the river. Here be many sheep. The path continues for a while before deciding to go upwards to a gate. Once through the gate you follow the path on the side of a slope to reach a kissing gate and come out on the main road. Turn LEFT and you are in the village of Aberdaron, and as it happens, the end of the Pilgrim's Way, at least the walking part of it. There remains the sea to be crossed to reach Bardsey Island. But not on foot, you'll be glad to know.

Aberdaron to Bardsey
Boat trip

A brisk boat trip and a meditative stroll on the untroubled island of Bardsey, the end of your pilgrimage.

First you need a boat. It is imperative you secure a booking for your boat trip before setting out on this excursion. These are the arrangements at the time of writing. Ring Colin on 07971 769 895 to make a booking. At present sailings [£30 return, 2015 prices] leave for the island *at 09.30, 10.30, 11.30 and occasionally 12.30. You have approximately 4 hours free time on the island. So, for example, if you leave at 11.30 you will arrive on the island at 12.00, leave at 16.00 and regain the mainland at 16.30.* Colin tells me he cancels, on average, two sailings out of seven in any one summer week, and often more during the autumn and winter months. Sailings depend on many factors such as wind speed and direction, tides, the strength of the current and wet or stormy conditions. You will be able to find out for certain if a sailing is going ahead by phoning again at *about 18.30 on the day before*, when Colin will confirm. Although conditions may seem to be favourable from your point of view, bear in mind that these may deteriorate as the day progresses, and the boatman will only sail to the island if he is convinced he will also be able to sail back on the same day! No one will be left stranded on the island, I am assured. However, if you wish to stay on the island beyond the one day, you should talk this through with Colin to fix your return trip. These arrangements may well change over time, *so double check.*

To reach the boat, drive to Cwrt, where there is a car park, and walk down to the beach at Porth Meudwy. There may appear to be no boat in sight but one will appear shortly, never fear! Be aware that the boat is open to the elements, and you are advised to wear waterproof trousers as well as cagoule, hat etc. The boat crossing may also be through rough water. If you are walking, or coming by bus, take the Wales Coastal Path from Aberdaron to Port Meudwy.

Once on the island you can wander as you please. You may wish to climb onto Mynydd Enlli, or visit places of interest: the lighthouse, the old school, the chapel, the oratory, the Bird and Field Observatory and the ruins of the Abbey, which are sparse. There are excellent café facilities at Tŷ Pellaf, and public toilets in Plas Bach yard. More details of what you can see and do on the island can be found in the booklet *Exploring Bardsey* (available from: www.bardsey.org/english/shop/shop.htm).

The Pilgrim's Way
Bardsey Island

Although there are signs of pre-Christian settlements on the island, St Cadfan is credited with building a monastery on Bardsey Island in the 6th century, soon to become the destination for pilgrims over the centuries. The 13th century Augustinian Abbey closed in 1537 on the dissolution of the monasteries and only a few remains of the tower can be seen today The lighthouse on the island opened in 1821. Bardsey Island still supports a farming and fishing community.

You will have time to yourself and an opportunity to reflect on the walk you have made in the steps of many pilgrims from Basingwerk Abbey to Bardsey Island. An idyllic conclusion.

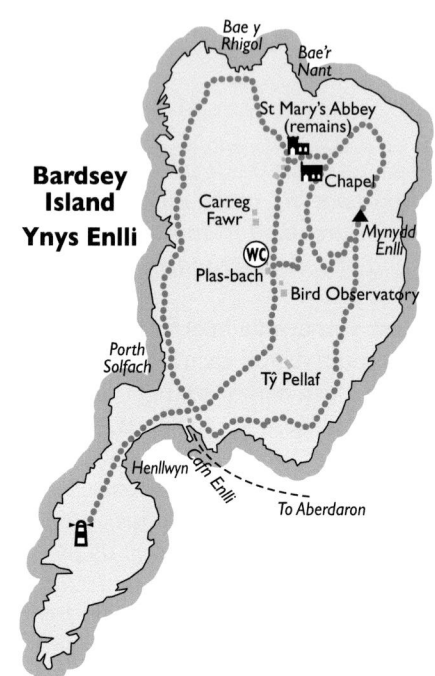

Bardsey Island – the end of the Way

Other long-distance trails available from Kittiwake

Borth to Strata Florida, Des Marshall
A long distance trail – and a pilgrimage
45 miles – £5.95 – ISBN 9781908748331

Ceredigion Coast Path, Liz Allan
The original guide, beautifully illustrated
60 miles – £4.95 – ISBN 9781902302676

The Conwy Valley Way, David Berry
The beautiful Conwy Valley from Conwy Bay to Llyn Conwy
102 miles – £8.95 – ISBN 9781902302461

The Dee Way, David Berry
From Prestatyn or Hoylake through Chester and Llangollen to the source near Dduallt mountain
142 miles – £8.95 – ISBN 9781908748218

Glyndŵr's Way National Trail, David Perrott
A fascinating exploration of the best of hidden Montgomeryshire, compiled with the cooperation of the Glyndŵr's Way manager
135 miles – £9.95 – ISBN 9781908748140

Llŷn Coastal Path, Des Marshall
One of the great British scenic coastal walks
97 Miles – £9.95 – ISBN 9781908748263

The Mawddach-Ardudwy Trail, David Berry
Starting from the beautiful Mawwdach estuary and linking the ancient upland and coastal areas of Ardudwy, linking Barmouth, Dolgellau, Porthmadog and Harlech
94 miles – £8.95 – ISBN 9781908748102

The Shropshire Way, David Berry
A beautiful walk exploring this recently upgraded trail linking Shrewsbury with Whitchurch, Oswestry, Ludlow and Little Wenlock
292 miles – £12.95 – ISBN 9781908748317

KITTIWAKE

Walks guides which detail superb routes
in most parts of Wales.

From Anglesey and Llandudno to the Brecon Beacons,
and from Machynlleth and Welshpool to Pembrokeshire and the Llŷn,
and including the borders, they offer a range
of carefully researched routes with something for all abilities.

Each guide has been compiled and written by a
dedicated author who really knows their particular area.

They are all presented in the **KITTIWAKE** clear
and easy-to-use style

For latest details of the expanding range, visit:

www.kittiwake-books.com

KITTIWAKE
3 Glantwymyn Village Workshops
Glantwymyn, Machynlleth
Montgomeryshire SY20 8LY